"I have worked closely with Rose for 25 years and I can attest to the fact that she has lived what she has put down on paper. Her life and her ministry are the fruit of letting those tears that flowed in the night call her to the Master who has turned her mourning into joy. She knows what it means to fix her eyes on Jesus – the One who has authored and is perfecting her faith.

Joy Comes in the Morning has come for such a time as this—in the midst of a world gone crazy – chaos and confusion abound – where marriage and relationships are devastated by sin and are corrupted by a culture that has turned its back on God. In a time when the Bible has been wrenched out of context to fit one's moods and lifestyle, this is truly a timely word in a due season.

Joy Comes in the Morning is a comforting, helpful, scriptural road map for any wife, but especially for a hurting wife. No matter what your source of pain may be, there is a wealth of wisdom offered to you, a feasting table at which you can dine. It is truly help in time of trouble.

What you *will not* find is superficial, out of context, emotionally-charged platitudes. What you *will* find is sound, honest, biblical truth; help for an eternal soul; solid ground on which to stand.

I pray for you beloved wife, that you will put your whole heart into the principles outlined in this Bible study. There is buried treasure here. Search for it and you will find it, in the midst of trials, pain, and struggle there is a true and lasting joy no matter the circumstances you are facing. This is the testimony of countless saints who have put their trust in the Lord.

When Thou didst say, 'Seek My face,' my heart said to Thee, 'Thy face, O Lord, I shall seek.'"

Kathy Gallagher, Speaker, Author, Co-Founder
Pure Life Ministries

"There are many good Bible studies available these days, but few could be more effective than one written by a young Godly wife who lived through a difficult and destructive relationship and discovered God was more than enough to heal her marriage.

I have known Rose for many years as a friend and colleague. She is a living testimony of the application of the Biblical principles in this study, which she has practiced and shared for many years with those who have lost hope and struggled with forgiveness and restoration. You will be blessed and encouraged by her book!"

Marlowe Bulkley, Speaker, Author, Biblical Counselor
International Association of Biblical Counselors

"The world has given women a very distorted view of what marriage is supposed to be. The focus is all about our happiness and if we aren't happy then divorce is the solution. But Rose makes clear, God's will for marriage is not our happiness but our holiness. Rose encourages women when they are facing marital trials to focus on God's Word, His faithfulness, and His sovereignty knowing that everything God does is for our good and His glory. Our focus should not be on our present, temporary problems but rather God's sanctifying work and His eternal plan. Rose beautifully weaves her personal testimony of marital trials throughout the book showing the very real life application of God's Word in our struggles."

Dr. Georgia Purdom, Director of Answers for Women
Answers in Genesis

"Rose has walked faithfully with the Lord, by His grace and power, through serious trials early on in her marriage.

In this day and age, when many wives are tempted to give up on their husbands, their marriages, and sadly even their relationships with God, Rose chose to draw near to Jesus. As she did, He helped her to see the deceitfulness of sin both in her husband and in her own heart. Yet, through the Gospel, He amazingly did a work of healing in each of them and their marriage. Rose and Jeff's testimony is one such story of what God faithfully does as He stands in covenant with a husband and wife.

This Bible study will walk you through evidences of His faithfulness to those who look to Him as they walk through the darkest nights in their marriage and their own personal lives. As you open the scriptures, you will see the same truths and promises that upheld Rose and her husband during their time of conflict and betrayal.

Their story testifies to all that Jesus can do when we look to Him to help us overcome our unbelief and put our trust in Him for what only He can do. May you be greatly blessed and encouraged as you seek to apply God's Word and see one story after another of how God worked in His people's lives to turn their weeping into true joy!"

Camille Cates, Author, Biblical Counselor, Assistant Director
Healing Hearts Ministries International

Joy Comes

in the

Morning

ROSE COLÓN

A BIBLE STUDY FOR WOMEN
GOING THROUGH VARIOUS TRIALS

Joy Comes in the Morning:
A Bible Study for Women Going Through Various Trials

Library of Congress Control Number:
Trade Paperback ISBN: 978-0-9864114-1-0
Design by: Dustin Smith

Published by Alethia International Publications – Taylors, SC

Printed in the United States of America.

I dedicate this Bible study to my dear grandmother, Manuela Rodriguez. She taught me, by example, how to persevere in the Lord when trials come into a marriage. Even though weeping endured for a night, on May 1st, 1988, she entered the joy that comes in the morning when she went to be with her Beloved Jesus.

Table of Contents

Psalm 30:11-12

"You have turned for me my mourning into dancing;

*You have put off my sackcloth and clothed me
with gladness;*

*To the end that my glory may sing praise to you
and not be silent.*

O Lord, my God, I will give thanks to you forever."

Preface

"I, Rose, take thee Jeff to be my lawfully wedded husband. To have and to hold, from this day forward. For better, for worse. For richer, for poorer. In sickness or in health. To love and to cherish, 'til death do us part, according to God's holy ordinance; thereto I pledge my love to thee."

It was on May 4th, 1991 when I made this commitment to my dear husband and before the God I love. I had told myself when I was single, when I finally met 'Mr. Right' I would pledge my love to him in this way, come what may. As I stood before the presence of all my family members, friends, and co-workers, I truly meant every one of those words from the depths of my heart to my beloved spouse. He was the only one I wanted to spend my life with here on earth. Oh, how I had waited for this special moment. My mom and stepdad were equally excited that their thirty two year old daughter was FINALLY getting married to a man they had truly grown to love as a son. Everything was just perfect on that day. To this day, many people who attended the wedding still tell us, "We have never been to a wedding like yours. It was a day we will always remember."

As Jeff and I recited our wedding vows and were pronounced husband and wife, all my hopes and dreams were anchored in the belief that he would love and cherish me all the days of his life. We were on this journey together ready to face any challenge that life might throw at us. I remember thinking nothing could divide us as we stood side by side together as a team. We were invincible. In fact, on my wedding invitation I had printed *Matthew 19:6, "...Therefore what God has joined together, let not man separate."* Little did I know how God would test me early on in my marriage using those very words. He was about to take me on a spiritual journey that I would not have chosen for myself. A pathway that would be revealing, cleansing, and healing. In all honesty, I wasn't ready for what we were about to face. In fact, I would not have signed up for what God had in store for me. Especially, coming from a good home where I knew I was loved by my parents. I had a good job teaching in a hospital in Queens, New York, and a beautiful place to live in the suburbs of Long Island. But God knew what I needed to draw me unto Himself in a greater way and to do a deeper work of sanctification in my heart.

I believe most of us women go into marriage with a mindset that life will be problem free. Likewise, we believe our spouse will meet our list of expectations and all our heartfelt desires. However, what we will see as we journey together through this study is that we all have unrealistic and unbiblical expectations that God must purify in us, so that He can be glorified the way He desires. So, He will often use any trial we face to accomplish His kingdom purposes in us. For me it was the trial you are about to read in this study. For you it might be something else. Nevertheless, the Biblical principles you will read about in the next eight weeks will apply to your situation, whatever you might be personally facing. Allow the Holy Spirit to search your heart as we begin this excursion together.

Week One, Day 1, Monday

I Don't Understand.
What Happened?

A Personal Testimony

Immediately after Jeff and I returned home from our honeymoon, I did not understand what was happening to us. The man who I had just pledged my love to disappeared two weeks after we got back. Jeff was missing for several days with no way for me to get in touch with him. *I was completely at my wit's end.* I felt as if my heart was reeling to and fro similar to what is described in *Psalm 107:27,* especially when I found out from his older sister that Jeff had a past he never told me about. Because we had dated for a year and a half before our wedding, I thought I knew my husband. Nevertheless, in the first three years of our marriage, we were sitting in a terrible darkness because of the deception we were both in.

To my knowledge, Jeff was bound in the affliction and irons of a drug addiction that he had no control over because he had rebelled against the words of God and despised the counsel of the Most High in his life (*Psalm 107:10*). As a result, he was taken captive by his sin only to dwell in the shadow of death. Oh, how we needed God's divine intervention early on in our marriage. There was no other way out. As my husband has testified numerous times, he needed a greater power within him to break free, and for God to transform him into the man of God that He had purposed for his life. Likewise, I needed God to give me what I needed to love, forgive, and persevere in this marriage, while He broke the gates of bronze and cut the bars of iron (*Psalm 107:11*) in my husband's heart, of his desires, and of his will.

I struggled to understand why Jeff would choose to check out on me in this way. I desperately needed a biblical perspective on what we were going through because none of this made any sense. I thought to myself, "*This is not supposed to happen.*" To make matters worse, I believed all the lies I had been exposed to in romance novels and movies before I had a relationship with Christ. After all, Hollywood's portrayal of Prince Charming someday sweeping me off my feet is what every young girl dreams of experiencing. However, in one moment, my entire world had come crashing down. Suddenly, I was in a dark reality. I realized that I had been sold a lie from the world about romance, marriage, and living happily ever after. It seemed as if our marriage had turned into a living nightmare here on earth. There were countless nights of not knowing where my husband was or what he was doing. I often wondered if I would ever see him again, or if I would get a phone call from someone saying that he was arrested or was dead. These are the types of thoughts that plagued my mind like vultures buzzing around a dead carcass.

At the advice and counsel of my Pastor, Jeff sought healing and change through two programs early on in our marriage, but I could not understand why he wasn't being set free from this besetting sin. Why hadn't God answered my prayers? After a while, I lost all hope.

Jesus told his disciples in *John 8:34*, *"Most assuredly, I say to you, whoever commits sin is a slave of sin."*

Likewise, in *Romans 6:16*, the apostle Paul wrote, *"Do you know that to whom you present yourselves slaves to obey, you are that one's slaves whom you obey, whether of sin leading to death, or of obedience leading to righteousness?"*

James wrote, *"Let no one say when he is tempted, "I am tempted by God"; for God cannot be tempted by evil, nor does He Himself tempt anyone. But each one is tempted when he is drawn away by his own desires and enticed. Then, when desire has conceived, it gives birth to sin; and sin, when it is full-grown, brings forth death." (James 1:13-15)*

After three years of pleading with God in prayer that He would have mercy on Jeff and that he would come to a *genuine repentance that leads to salvation (2 Corinthians 7:10-11)*, my Pastor's final counsel was, *"Jeff must go to Kentucky into another program or else he will be removed from church membership until he repents."* (*Matthew 18:15-17*) "Another program?" was my response. "How many programs do we need to go through?" I realized that there was an all-out war going on for my husband's soul and our marriage.

At that moment, my heart and mind were flooded with so much confusion. You see, when I married Jeff, I thought I was marrying a Christian. After all, my husband was on the worship team, went to church faithfully, and complied with our Pastor's guidance and counsel. I failed to understand why a loving God could allow His daughter to experience such deep heartache and betrayal. Questions whirled around in my mind like, "Who can I talk to about what we were going through? How would it look if people found out what Jeff was doing? Why wasn't he happy? How could he take our marriage vows so lightly?" My heart was broken into a million pieces. No earthly being could mend or comfort me no matter how hard they tried.

Then the Lord laid it on a co-worker's heart to send me a scriptural passage. She did not know what I was going through, but she did know Jesus in a very personal and intimate way. As I arrived at the office that day, I opened her interoffice envelope. The following verses were written on a piece of paper from *Isaiah 54:4-6:*

> *"Do not fear, for you will not be ashamed; neither be disgraced, for you will not be put to shame; for you will forget the shame of your youth and will not remember the reproach of your widowhood anymore. For your Maker [is] your husband, The LORD of hosts [is] His name; and your Redeemer [is] the Holy One of Israel; He is called the God*

of the whole earth. For the LORD has called you like a woman forsaken and grieved in spirit, like a youthful wife when you were refused," says your God."

Through God's Word, I realized that He saw and knew everything we were going through. The sleepless nights, the despair in my heart, and all my questions. God sympathized with me and wanted to comfort me through all of this. He was not angry with me. Rather, His heart was full of compassion. His desire was to draw me to Himself to reveal His heart to me in a more intimate way. Oh, how I needed to know my Heavenly Father in this way as I was walking on this pathway with my husband.

What is amazing is how God used my husband's sin to get our attention, because He was after *both* of our hearts. He wanted us to get our misplaced desires off of one another. We were looking to each other to meet our needs and make us happy. Meanwhile, the Creator of the universe was calling for both of us to look to Him as the only source of life. He is the One who can be to us what our spouse cannot. I had to consider that while we have our existence here on earth, these relationships are temporary. However, our relationship with the Lord is eternal. As I began to see this situation through the lens of scripture, I slowly realized the blessing of this trial. Jeff's sin had invaded my comfort zone. But when I could see the hand of God during it, I was able to submit to Christ's will for our lives, regardless of how painful the process would be.

Dear one, you might be thinking, just as I did early on in my marriage, I don't understand what has happened to my husband and me. I thought I knew who I was marrying but I hardly know who he is. Please take some time to write out a prayer, some specific thoughts, or questions you have as you pour out your heart before God in the space below. He is there waiting for you to turn to Him as a wife who has been forsaken and grieved in spirit.

"The LORD is near to those who have a broken heart and saves such as have a contrite spirit." (Psalm 34:18)

Beloved, these words are very true. Let Him reveal His heart to you during this difficult time in your life.

Week One, Day 2, Tuesday

How Can Any Good
Come Out of Our Mess?

1. Read *Luke 22:31-34*

In this passage of scripture, Jesus told Peter, *"Satan has
asked for you, that he may sift you as wheat. But I have
prayed for you, that your faith should not fail."*

2. What did Jesus instruct Peter to do after he had
    gone through this refining process?

       Jesus knew Peter would utterly fail Him by
denying Him three times during His arrest, as we see in
John 18:15-27. Yet, because God is all-knowing (*Psalm
139* and *Jeremiah 23:24*), He also knew the significant
role Peter would play in church history and the future
blessing he would be to the Body of Christ. I am sure at

the time of Peter's denial, he could have never imagined God would bring anything good out of his forsaking Christ. But, He did.

What about the life of Joseph in *Genesis chapters 37; 39, and 40?* In *Genesis 37:3-4,* Joseph was seventeen years old and was deeply hated by his brothers because their father loved him the most (*verses 3-4*). They hated the dreams Joseph would have (*verses 5, 8, 11*) and conspired to see how they could kill him (*verse 18*). Stripped of his tunic and cast into a pit in the wilderness to die (*verses 22-24*), Joseph was sold into slavery to the Midianites. He was then taken to Egypt and purchased by Potiphar, an officer and captain of the guards of Pharaoh (*verses 26-36*). Later, in *Genesis 39:7-20,* Joseph was unjustly accused of rape by Potiphar's wife and put into prison. In *Genesis 40:14, 23* Joseph was forgotten in prison by the chief butler who promised to get him out. For two full years Joseph had to wait for God to rescue him (*Genesis 41:1*).

3. Read *Psalm 105:17-22.* What upheld Joseph during this time of difficulty?

This word *"tested"* describes the smelting process, which removes dross from fine metal. It is a purification process, which we also see in *Psalm 66:10-12*,

> *"For **You**, O God, have tested us; **You** have refined us as silver is refined. **You** brought us into the net; **You** laid affliction on our backs, **You** have caused men to ride over our heads; we went through fire and through water, But **You** brought us out to rich fulfillment."*

As we look at the life of Joseph, at the end of his refining process God promoted him at the age of thirty years old to be the second most powerful man in Egypt. I'm sure while Joseph was going through this time of testing that he might have had a moment when he asked, *"How can any good come out of this mess?"* Dear one, you might be asking yourself that very question. I tell you the truth: God can absolutely bring much good out of all you are facing at this moment. *Romans 8:28-29* tells us,

> *"And we know that all things work for good to those who love God, to those who are called according to His purpose. For whom He foreknew, He also predestined to be conformed to the image of His Son, that He might be the firstborn among many brethren."*

Beloved, hold onto that promise and may the testimony of these two dear saints, Peter and Joseph, encourage your heart today.

Week One, Day 3, Wednesday

God's Purpose for Affliction In Our Lives

Many times, when we face different trials in our marriage, the human tendency is to blame someone else for our sinful behavior. At times, we can even blame the devil for everything that happens to us *(Genesis 3:14)*. At other times, we can blame God just as Adam did when Eve sinned in the Garden of Eden *(Genesis 3:9-12)*. While it is true that we do have an enemy, who desires to destroy the testimony and image of God in marriage, the Bible teaches us that God is still sovereign and in control of everything that comes our way. We see that in the life of Job.

1. Read *Job 1:1* through *Job 2:10.*

2. Summarize everything Job experienced.

3. As you recall *Job 1:8-12* and *Job 2:1-7*, who was in control and behind this sifting process in his life?

4. Read *Job 42:1-6*. What was God's purpose for this affliction in Job's life?

5. What revelation did Job have about himself and about God at the end of his suffering?

6. Do you think this knowledge of Job's heart and of God could have happened any other way?

7. In *Job 42:10-17,* we have a testimony of how God brought good out of all the trials that Job faced. What stands out to you the most?

Beloved, God's purpose for affliction in our lives can be summed up by this quote by Elizabeth Elliot, *"Every assignment is measured and controlled by God for my eternal good."* Be encouraged my friend! Even though your world may have been turned upside down, God is still in control. As we have read in today's study, He has a divine purpose for everything you are going through.

Week One, Day 4, Thursday

Having a Kingdom Mindset In Your Trial

1. Read *Hebrews 11*

As we read about the heroes of the faith, we learn God's people are not exempt from affliction. In fact, we see this throughout the Bible, as well as in our present church age. Many of God's saints have faced *"torture, trials of cruel mocking and scourging, bonds and imprisonment, they were stoned, sawn in two, tempted, slain with the sword, they wandered about in sheepskins and goatskins, being destitute, afflicted and tormented, they wandered in deserts and in mountains, and in dens and caves of the earth." (Hebrews 11:35-40)* How were these saints able to endure such things?

The insight we glean from *Hebrews 11* is that Abraham and many others had a kingdom mindset that enabled them to follow God wherever He was leading. They were not living for this world nor the things of this world. In fact, *Hebrews 11:10* tells us,

> *"God's saints waited for the city which has foundations, whose builder and maker is God.*

29

They confessed that they were strangers and pilgrims on the earth (verse 13), they were seeking a homeland, a heavenly country, therefore God is not ashamed to be called their God, for He has prepared a city for them (verses 14-16)."

These dear saints were willing to go through the toughest of times because their love for God was far greater than the love of their lives in this world. *(Revelation 12:11)*

Throughout many years of counseling women, I have observed that the crises they face are what they are treasuring in their hearts above their love for God. This could be a perfect marriage, a perfect husband, the perfect kids, the perfect job, the perfect house, the perfect image, or the American dream. Our basic mindset, without us even realizing it, can be to *let **my** kingdom come, let **my** will be done.* What we fail to realize is that trials have a way of showing us how earthly minded we really are. God revealed this to my worldly heart through my husband's sin. It was very humbling to recognize how I was living for this world and not thinking about eternity.

2. Look up *Matthew 6:21*. Write out what Jesus said about our hearts and what we treasure.

3. If you were to take an honest inventory of your life in comparison with the heroes of faith, what would God write about you?

4. Where would He say your treasure is?

Many times, we struggle to understand why God would allow various hardships into our marriage. But God uses them to set our hearts on eternity, if we let Him. He will also use trials to show us the other loves we treasure in our heart. Although it is quite painful to look at, He does it because He is jealous for all our affections (*James 4:5*). His desire is that we, *"love Him with **all** of our heart, **all** of our mind and **all** of our strength." (Matthew 22:37)* As we have this kingdom mindset, we will be able to endure hardships just as these heroes of faith did until the very end, whatever that end may be.

Week One, Day 5, Friday

Personal Application

Review Days 1 through 4 of this week's study and answer the following questions.

1. What do you believe about God when He allows trials to come into your life?

2. Do you believe God can bring good out of what you are going through? If so, why? (Use scriptures to support your answer.)

3. Describe how this trial has captured your attention.

4. As you live from day to day, what indicators can you list that reveal you are more consumed with your life in this world verses eternity?

5. Would you say that you need more of a kingdom mindset in your trial? If so, how would that look in your daily life?

Healing Balm
For Your Shattered Heart

A Personal Testimony

As you are walking through your current trial, you may be wondering, "Could there possibly be healing balm for my broken heart that has been shattered by disappointment? After all, I thought I knew what I was getting into when I married my husband. However, what I had hoped for has not turned out in the way I had believed. It seems as if with every expectation I have, my husband has repeatedly let me down. Likewise, it is so frustrating for me to know what he is struggling with because he does not communicate with me. I have no idea what is going on inside of him. Sometimes it is like pulling teeth to get more than a one-word answer from him. I feel so terribly alone in this marriage. I just don't understand how we wound up this way?"

As I shared in Week One, Day 1 of this study, what a comfort it was to my heart when God revealed to me *Isaiah 54:4-6* through my co-worker. To know that the Creator of the universe, who upholds all things by the power of His Word (*Hebrews 1:3*), was speaking to me through the scriptures during my despair and confusion. His words brought such a healing balm to my shattered heart. What the Psalmist declared in *Psalm 119:25, "My soul clings to the dust; revive me according to Your Word,"* is exactly how I felt as I was walking through this trial. I was clinging to the dust of despair and hopelessness. I needed God's Word to revive me in the midst of all that we were facing. It is amazing, how the Word of God was providing a comfort to me and giving me life (*Psalm 119:50)* while Jeff and I were sitting in the valley of the shadow of death.

My Pastor played an instrumental role in this difficult journey. Whenever I would call him to tell him Jeff was missing in action, his counsel to me was, "Rose, get in the Bible, pray for God's wisdom, and He will show you what to do." It seemed as if whenever I turned to the scriptures for comfort or hope I would find a word of encouragement and healing. There were even times when the Holy Spirit would gently rebuke or bring a correction to my heart when I needed it. I started to realize that in God's sovereignty, "*It was good for me that I had been afflicted, that I may learn His statutes." (Psalm 119:75)* God knew how necessary it was for me to learn His precepts while I was going through this ordeal with my husband. Through this trial, I am thankful that Jesus was very gentle in showing me my sins and my need for repentance.

As I spent time reading the Holy Scriptures and in prayer, the Holy Spirit revealed to me how God required me to learn how to love as Christ loves, even while my husband was in sin and my heart was hurting *(John 15:12)*. I had to be taught how to forgive in the way Jesus told Peter in *Luke 17:4*. I had to practice having a grateful heart by not murmuring or complaining to others about my spouse *(1 Thessalonians 5:18)*. Moreover, I needed to master respecting my mate whenever I felt he did not deserve my respect *(Ephesians 5:33)*. I had come to realize God desired to change me while Jeff and I were going through this trial. The Holy Spirit began to show me how much I needed Jesus to touch the inside world of my heart just as much as my husband did. As *Psalm 107:20* so beautifully testifies, *"He sent His Word and healed them and delivered them from their destructions"* is exactly what the Great Physician wanted to do in me through all we were facing.

Likewise, your Beloved Christ will speak His words of comfort and life to you just as He did for so many other individuals we read about in the gospels when they turned to Him. Lives that were completely shattered with nowhere else to turn were never let down by our dear, Savior who was moved with compassion towards them. Talk to Jesus about all the betrayal and hurt you are experiencing. Give Him your distresses, troubles, frustrations, and burdens. Be willing to be intimate with your Creator in this way. He already knows all you are wrestling with.

> *Psalm 51:17* tells us, *"The sacrifices of God are a broken spirit, a broken and a contrite heart, these, O God, You will not despise."*

37

This word *broken* used in this passage comes from the Hebrew word *shabar*, which means *to break, to break in pieces, to break in or down, to rend violently, to rupture, to be maimed, to be crippled, to be wrecked, to be crushed*, and *to be shattered*. Dear one, does this describe the current condition of your heart? I know it did mine when I found out about my husband's sin. God used my husband's transgression to show me what Isaiah stated about God in *Isaiah 55:8-9*,

> *"For My thoughts are not your thoughts; nor are your ways, My ways" says the Lord. "For as the heavens are higher than the earth, so are My ways higher than your ways, and My thoughts than your thoughts."*

I have found this to be true in the lives of many women over the years of my ministry. God works in ways which we would never choose for ourselves. But, when we embrace them, it is amazing to see what He does inside of us to make us more like His Son. That is His goal.

> *"For whom He foreknew, He also predestined to be conformed to the image of His Son, that He might be the firstborn among many brethren."* *(Romans 8:29)* May these precious words become a healing balm for your broken heart.

As we consider what our precious Redeemer said about Himself when He was handed the book of the Prophet Isaiah in the synagogue on the Sabbath Day. He began to read,

"The Spirit of the Lord is upon Me, because He has anointed Me to preach the gospel to the poor; He has sent Me to heal the broken-hearted, to proclaim liberty to the captives and recovery of sight to the blind, to set a liberty to those who are oppressed; to proclaim the acceptable year of the Lord." Then He closed the book, gave it back to the attendant and sat down. Jesus declared to them, *"Today this Scripture is fulfilled in your hearing."* (Luke 4:16-21)

My friend, Jesus is your Great Physician, as well as the healing ointment you so desperately need for your shattered heart. His desire is to fulfill what we read in these verses in your life in the midst of all you are facing with your husband. The Lord Jesus is what you need.

Ask the Lord to protect your heart from becoming hardened because of the trial God has permitted to enter your marriage. Allow Him to draw you near to Him in your brokenness. Cling to Christ with every fiber of your being, no matter how long it takes for your husband to come into *a godly sorrow which produces repentance leading to salvation. (2 Corinthians 7:11)* There is so much more He yearns to do in you through all you are facing. Guard against limiting your wonderful Savior by focusing on your husband's sin, how he has hurt you, or what your marriage lacks. Let your testimony be what we read in the Song of Solomon, *"Who is this coming up from the wilderness, leaning upon her beloved?"* (Song of Solomon 8:5) Why don't you take some time, at this moment, to lean into the sweet arms of Jesus? As you do, He will pour out the healing ointment of His Word into every crack and crevice of your heart.

May the cry of your heart be, *"Let him kiss me with the kisses of his mouth, for your love is better than wine. Because of the fragrance of your good ointments, your name is ointment poured forth; therefore, the virgins love you. Draw me away! We (I) will run after you. The king has brought me into his chambers."* (Song of Solomon 1:2-4)

Shut yourself into your prayer chamber often as you walk through this valley of despair. As you do, the King of Glory will come into your heart in a greater way to do what He proclaimed in *Luke 4:16-21. "He is the same yesterday, today and forever." (Hebrews 13:8)* May this be your testimony, and may you find the healing balm you are longing for 'in Christ alone.' He will never disappoint you.

Write out a prayer in the space below to the Great Physician.

Drawing Near to God

Throughout the Bible from the book of *Genesis* to *The Revelation of Jesus Christ,* we see how God's heart yearns for intimate fellowship with us. So much so, that He sent His Only Begotten Son into the world to die for all of mankind. As His desire was to restore the fellowship Adam and Eve had with Him before they had sinned in the Garden of Eden (See *Genesis 2 and John 3:16).* This act of kindness beautifully reflects His longing heart. It is amazing how God will use everything we go through to draw us to Himself.

However, what I have observed in counseling is the tendency for a wife to run to and fro looking for comfort and answers from any available source she can find, instead of looking to God for answers. In her desperate attempt to find solace, some women have turned to the world and various mind-altering drugs or substances. Some have even fallen into the trap of pouring out their hearts to a person of the opposite sex only to find themselves in a situation they never thought was possible. It is just in our nature, when we are in trouble, to go to one of these earthly resources rather than to God and His Word. But when we look at David's life story, he is such a biblical example of where to turn when your whole world is being turned upside down. What we learn from David is that no matter what his circumstances were, he drew near to God.

As you read some of the Psalms that David wrote, make these observations: (1) What was he going through, (2) What inner turmoil was he facing, and (3) How did he turn to God during that time?

1. *Psalm 3*

2. *Psalm 13*

3. *Psalm 27*

4. *Psalm 30*

5. *Psalm 34:1-10*

As David drew near to God, we can see the confidence he had in Him even during his trials and the inner struggles he faced. It didn't matter what the situation was. David made sure he did not lose sight of the attributes of God. As David rehearsed the goodness and mercy of God in his life, he found the comfort his soul needed time and time again. What about you? Are you learning how to lean on God's everlasting arms through what you are facing just as David did? If so, write out how God is using your trial to teach you how to do this?

6. Read *Matthew 11:28-30.* Write out Jesus' invitation to you today.

Week Two, Day 3, Wednesday

A Look at Your Heavenly Father's Heart

When a trial comes into a marriage there is a tendency to lose sight of who God is in the midst of everything a couple is facing. Many times, a wife has become so beaten down by her husband's sin that she is unable to believe what God has said about Himself. Her circumstances tend to cloud out and eclipse the realities of God's nature and sovereignty. I have found that just as Jesus had to constantly remind His disciples of the Father's heart, we too, need frequent reminders.

As you read the following verses, ask the Holy Spirit to make God's Word personal to you. Write out what He reveals to you about your Father's heart.

1. *Deuteronomy 31:6, 8*

2. *Nehemiah 9:16-21*

44

3. *Psalm 9:9-10*

4. *Isaiah 43:1-3*

5. *2 Corinthians 1:3-4*

6. *Romans 8:31-39*

Beloved, even though the storm clouds of life might have eclipsed who God is or caused you to doubt if He is with you, your Abba Father has not left you to do this by yourself. You can believe, trust, rely on, and have confidence in the Holy Scriptures and what God has said about Himself. He is your place of refuge. What we read in *Proverbs 18:10* is reality,

"The name of the Lord is a strong tower, the righteous run into it and they are safe."

Please take some time right now to express your love and gratitude to Him for all He is and desires to be to you through this trial. Write out ten things you are thankful for in the space provided below.

Finding Comfort in the Word

As we seek to find comfort in the Word of God, let us look at *"The Word (Jesus) who was in the beginning with God and who was God." (John 1:1)* The apostle John wrote in *John 1:14, "And the Word (Jesus) became flesh and dwelt among us, and we beheld His glory, as of the only begotten of the Father, full of grace and truth."* In the Strong's Concordance, the Greek word for *dwell* is *skenoo*, which means *to tent or to occupy (as a mansion), to reside or to have or fix one's tabernacle, to abide or to live, to dwell,* just as God did in the Tabernacle that we read about in the Old Testament.

When you consider that the God of our universe would come down to earth to reveal Himself to mankind through His Son, Jesus Christ, knowing what it would cost Him is simply mind-boggling. You can understand why David would pen in *Psalm 144:3, "What is man, that You take knowledge of him? Or the son of man, that You are mindful of him?"* Jesus knew He was coming into a world that would hate *(John 7:7; John 15:18)*, despise and reject *(Isaiah 53:3)*, and eventually kill Him *(Mark 10:34)*. Yet, He still chose to tabernacle among us. Why? Let us look at the following scriptures to see if we can answer that question.

1. *Isaiah 53:3-12*

2. *Hebrews 2:17-18*

3. *Hebrews 4:14-16*

Aren't you thankful, '*The Word made flesh*' came down from heaven so He could sympathize with us throughout our pilgrimage here on earth? These passages of scripture show us this truth. It is at His throne room of mercy and grace where we find the comfort we are seeking for all the trials we will face in our lifetime. Whenever we turn away from everything else and turn to Him in this way, He ministers to those places in our hearts where no other earthly being ever could. As the Psalmist declared,

"Deep calls unto deep at the noise of Your waterfalls; all Your waves and billows have gone over me." (Psalm 42:7)

Even though the deep waters of your trial may be churning around and sweeping over you, you can hope in God to provide the comfort you need right in the very midst of all you are facing.

4. Read *Romans 15:4.* How else is God's Word a comfort to us?

God's Word speaks to us of all the saints who have gone before us. Their lives reveal to mankind God's desire for us to turn to Him as our source of comfort and hope. It is my prayer you will find the solace you are longing for as you spend time in God's Holy Word and with His Beloved Son throughout this Bible study, my dear friend.

Week Two, Day 5, Friday

Personal Application

Review Days 1 through 4 of this week's study and answer the following questions.

1. Who do you tend to run to when you are facing inner turmoil or a trial?

2. In which specific area of your life does God desire for you to lean on Him?

3. Based on your Day 3 homework, what are some practical things you can do to get your eyes on God during difficult times?

4. Write out how you can begin turning to God and His Word when you are in distress.

5. Do you really believe Jesus has what you need when no other resource is available to you? If not, why not?

Understanding
The Root of Sin

A Personal Testimony

Throughout my years of counseling couples, I have seen that many times a husband and wife do not understand why there is so much turmoil going on in their marriage, especially when they are professing Christians. It is in those times that my husband and I have to examine this couple's faith and their relationship with God, especially if there is no evidence of the fruit of the Spirit within their marriage. This was something Jeff and I had to do ourselves when we started meeting as a couple with our Pastors. This trial had caused both of us *to examine ourselves to see if we were even in the faith,* as the apostle Paul tells us to do so in *2 Corinthians 13:5.*

In all honesty, it wasn't until this happened for my husband and me that everything began to make sense to me. Deep within my heart I could not figure out why my husband kept going back to living a selfish lifestyle in using drugs if the Bible states in *2 Corinthians 5:17, "If anyone is in Christ, he is a new creation; old things have passed away: behold, all things have become new."* If Jeff had truly been born again, where was the new life the scriptures promised? Why did his sin still have dominion over him when the apostle Paul proclaimed in *Romans 6:14, "Sin shall not have dominion over you, for you are not under the law but under grace?"* Something was very wrong. Likewise, I couldn't understand why I would respond to him in such an unchristlike manner. We needed a miracle to happen in both of us.

My pastor's wife encouraged me to continue in prayer to God. My leaders were just as baffled as to why Jeff continued to be enslaved to his addiction. They had decided to meet with Jeff to find out why he kept *choosing* to go back. During the meeting, my husband finally confessed everything. Immediately afterward, the leadership met with me. They discovered we were not only dealing with Jeff's addiction to crack cocaine, but he would occasionally be involved in sexual sin while under the influence of drugs.

> *1 John 1:5-6* states, *"This is the message which we declared to you, that God is light and in Him is no darkness at all. If we say that we have fellowship with Him, and walk in darkness, we lie and do not practice the truth."*

My heart was devastated. Who was this man who committed before God to love, protect, and care for me until death do us part? Our marriage had been a lie from the very beginning. It was so hard to face this reality. I thought I married a Christian man.

After three years of fighting this battle, I was ready to file for a divorce. It seemed as if nothing was working for us. I thought leaving my husband would be the only way to end this nightmare. To make matters worse I had Christian women telling me, "You don't deserve this; Jeff doesn't appreciate someone like you; why don't you just divorce him?" There was even one-time when Jeff's father told me, "If my son does not get his act together, you should leave him!"

There were so many voices to sort through, not to mention the voice of the enemy telling me, "You've failed Jeff as a wife; he doesn't want to be married to you." It was such a terrible darkness that seemed to haunt me day and night. I was so confused. I could not think straight. I had no idea what to do. I was afraid of putting my hope in anything changing only to have it dashed to pieces again.

Although I was experiencing much inner turmoil, the Lord put the right people in my life. God knew I needed these folks to help me work through my emotional roller coaster by teaching me how to respond biblically. God had surrounded me with godly men and women who spoke biblical truth into my life rather than their opinions. They were the instruments He used to help lift my head when the bottom was dropping out from under me. So much gratitude fills my heart to this day knowing they were standing with me through all of this. Jesus was able to reveal His unconditional love to us through each one of these dear saints. It was through their obedience to God that I began to have such a glimpse of God's love that melted my heart with compassion for what my husband was wrestling with.

After much prayer, my Pastor decided to implement *Matthew 18:15-17* by telling my husband if he continued in his sin, he could not be in fellowship with the church body. His only other option was to go to Pure Life Ministries in Kentucky. I knew we both needed this time apart. That time would help me to sort through some of my own inner struggles. Jesus was showing me I had some decisions to make as well.

The Holy Spirit gently challenged me by asking, "Are you willing to follow God with or without your husband?" I had no idea if Jeff would find true repentance at Pure Life Ministries. I mean, after all, this was his third program. However, deep within my heart I knew there was no other option for me but to continue to go forward in my relationship with the Lord, whether I was married or not. This was a pivotal fork in the road for me.

What I had come to realize was that we both needed to make a deeper consecration to the Lord and to allow Him to use this trial to separate our hearts from out of this world unto Himself in a greater way. As Jesus said in *Matthew 6:24* and *in Luke 16:13,*

> *"No man (no servant) can serve two masters for either he will hate the one and love the other; or else he will hold to the one and despise the other. You cannot serve God and mammon."*

At the root of Jeff's betrayal was his divided heart. I could not take it personally. John Piper, a well know Christian author, has said it in this way: *"Sin is what we do when we are not satisfied in God."*

Jeff was trying to serve God while he still desired to live for this world and all it had to offer. Being an elevator mechanic for all the boroughs of New York City, my husband made a decent salary. However, his job took him right into all the areas where it would be easy for him to act out his sin. My Pastor would tell Jeff he needed to resign from his job. Despite my Pastor's counsel, Jeff would always have a better plan, which we knew in the end would fail, just as the scriptures tell us, *"There is a way that seems right to a man, but the end of that way is death." (Proverbs 14:25; 16:25)*

The apostle John told us in *1 John 2:15-17,*

"Do not love the world or the things in the world. If anyone loves the world, the love of the Father is not in him. For all that is in the world – the lust of the flesh, the lust of the eyes, and the pride of life- is not of the Father but is of the world. And the world is passing away, and the lust of it; but he who does the will of God abides forever."

This is what was at the heart of my husband's bondage. He needed to love and surrender to God rather than to this world and all it had to offer.

My husband had to *find and do God's will for his life,* which would be the only *way out for him.* That could only happen by having an abiding relationship with God through His Son Jesus Christ and spending time in His Word daily. Jesus said in *John 8:31-32,*

> *"If you abide in My word, you are My disciples indeed. And you shall know the truth and the truth shall make you free."*

As Jeff would spend time in the Bible, the Holy Spirit could bring correction into his life by showing him how he was not *presenting his body as a living sacrifice, holy, and acceptable to God which was his reasonable service,* as a true disciple of Christ *(Romans 12:1).* It was only then that he could begin to find true freedom.

Pure Life Ministries would be the vehicle that God could use to help us to grow in our relationship with Christ in this way, as well as, to build spiritual disciplines into our lives which we also needed. The question then became, were we going to surrender and be obedient to God, so His will could be done in and through our marriage?

After we made that commitment, we began to experience what a dear friend once told me, **"God can take the worst thing that has ever happened to you and make it as though it never happened."** Twenty-seven years later, I can say that God can if we surrender to His way of living. Beloved, God can break every chain of bondage in our lives as we, *"Walk in the Spirit; we shall* *not fulfill the lust of the flesh if we crucify the flesh with its passions and desires."* *(Galatians 5:16, 24)* This is accomplished moment-by-moment.

What are some questions you may have about your husband's sin that you would like to speak with your spiritual leaders about? Why don't you write them down in the space below?

Understanding
The War Within

In *Jeremiah 17:9-10*, we have a description of the condition of the human heart apart from Christ. Jeremiah stated, *"The heart is deceitful above all things, and desperately wicked; who can know it? I, the Lord, search the heart, I test the mind, even to give every man according to his ways, according to the fruit of his doings."* It is difficult for a wife to understand how she could be married to her husband while he lives a life of deception while they are both under the same roof.

But take a moment to consider the heart of a child. Think about the times you may have had to confront him or her about something which the evidence proves the child's guilt. However, when you ask them if they committed such an act, they lie to you. Did you ever wonder who taught them how to be so deceptive in trying to cover up their sin? No one. In fact, from the very beginning, when Adam and Eve sinned in the Garden of Eden, they tried to hide from God what they had done by covering themselves with fig leaves (*Genesis 3:7-11*). What we see from *Romans 3:10-14* is true, *"There is none righteous, no not one...there is none who does good, no, not one...their throat is an open tomb; with their tongues they have practiced deceit, the poison of asps is under their lips whose mouth is full of cursing and bitterness."* That is not a pretty picture of the human heart, is it?

When a wife is trying to sort through her reasoning and emotions as to why her husband is choosing to sin against her, she needs to understand that there is a war waging within.

Look up the scriptures below and answer the following questions.

1. Read *Matthew 15:18-20* and *Mark 7:15-23.* Where do sinful actions come from?

2. According to *John 8:34*, what happens to a person who commits habitual sin?

3. Read *Romans 7:15-24*. What stands out to you the most about this passage of scripture?

4. Read *Galatians 5:17*. How can you relate this scripture towards your spouse's struggle?

5. What are the works of the flesh or sinful nature that are listed in *Galatians 5:19-21*?

My dear sister, God's Word helps us to see where the real problem lies. It is through these passages we see how desperately we need what Jesus did for us on the cross. Without the cross, there would be no hope for any of us. The reality is, Christ alone can break the dominion of sin in your spouse's life.

Please take some time to pray *Psalm 51* for your husband. Ask God to grant your mate a repentant heart just as He did for King David. Only God can bring about this kind of godly sorrow. He alone can uproot your spouse's sin problem and bring about the true repentance your husband needs and that you long for him to experience.

What the World Tells Women

As we reflect on yesterday's homework, we see why a biblical understanding of the war within is so important for a wife. The reason being, our world will tend to blame a wife for her husband's sinful behavior. But when we look at the heart (not just the behavior) through the lens of the scriptures, we see a very different story.

I remember a women's event in which I was asked to speak. A dear lady came up to me in tears to tell me her story. It was heartbreaking. She began to tell me all the surgeries she had endured to satisfy her husband's unbridled lusts. She had succumbed to his desires thinking, "If I become what he is exposing himself to, he no longer will give in to his sin." How wrong she was. In tears she told me the regret she had and to make matters worse, her husband was still in unrepentant sin. I just wanted to weep with her. How many women have fallen into this web of lies? Our world inundates us with the message of how we need to look, dress, and perform to be the objects of men's desires. The lies our society promotes about women and their bodies can cause a female to become very self-absorbed, self-focused, and self-centered. Women then compare themselves to other women, wishing God had created them differently.

1. Read *Psalm 139:13-18.* Do you believe what God's Word says about you? Why or why not?

2. Look up the Hebrew word *marvelous* in a Strong's Concordance and write out its definition.

3. According to *1 Corinthians 6:19-20,* to whom do our bodies belong to?

4. Read *Romans 12:1-2*. What are we told to do with
   our bodies?

In the Amplified Bible *Romans 12:1-2* reads, *"I
appeal to you, therefore, brethren, and beg of you in view
of (all) the mercies of God, to make a decisive dedication
of your bodies (presenting all your member and facilities)
as a living sacrifice, holy (devoted, consecrated) and well
pleasing to God, which is your reasonable (rational,
intelligent) service and spiritual worship. Do not be
conformed to this world (this age), (fashioned after and
adapted to its external, superficial customs), but be
transformed (changed) by the (entire) renewal of your
mind (by its new ideals and its new attitude), so that you
may prove (for yourselves) what is the good and
acceptable and perfect will of God even the thing which is
good and acceptable and perfect (in His sight for you).*

Contrary to what our culture tells us, Christian
women need to renew their minds with God's Word in this
area of their lives. Just as *Psalm 139:14* states, *"we are
fearfully and wonderfully made"* because we are God's
creation formed in His image and likeness (*Genesis 1:26-
27*). If we have been born again, the Holy Spirit has taken
up residence in our bodies and they now belong to God.
Take some time this week to meditate on these passages

66

of scripture. You might want to write them out on an index card and post them up in prominent places to hide God's Word in your heart. Ask the Holy Spirit to help you to believe what God has said about you instead of listening to the lies of this world. Your husband is choosing to sin not because of what you are not, my friend; rather he's doing this because of what is in his heart. For God has said, "*you are fearfully and wonderfully made.*"

Renewing Our Mind With the Word of God

The spirit of this world is constantly promoting a hedonistic message about our lives in this world that is contrary to the Word of God. In fact, everywhere we turn we are bombarded with the message that this life is all about pleasure, entertainment, acquiring more and more material possessions, our social status, and keeping the outward person young and fit. All of this is contrary to what God has said is more important. On a daily basis we are assaulted with the temptation to yield to the lust of the flesh, the lust of the eyes, and the pride of life, which is why we must renew our minds with the Word of God day and night. When we do this, we can discern what is correct biblical thinking versus what is worldly thinking. So then meditating on the scriptures is crucial for what we think will trigger feelings; based on those feelings we will act either in a biblical way or sinful way. To see how this plays itself out, let's go back to the Garden of Eden.

1. Read through *Genesis 2:16-18* and *Genesis 3:1-6.*

2. Write out "what God had actually said" verse by verse. Then write out "how Eve quoted what God had said" verse by verse.

3. Please use *Genesis 3:1-6* to answer this question: How was Eve's thinking, feelings, and actions influenced when she chose to dwell on satan's offer which ultimately lead her to disobey what God had said?

So many different temptations come at us that can influence our thinking and what we choose in those times only exposes what we treasure in our hearts more than God. Remember, whenever we stray from the truth of God's Word, there are always consequences as Adam and Eve quickly discovered. *(Genesis 3:14-19)*

> *2 Timothy 3:16-17* states, *"All Scripture is given by inspiration of God, and is profitable for doctrine, for reproof, for correction, for instruction in righteousness, that the man of God may be complete, thoroughly equipped for every good work."*

> Likewise *Psalm 12:6* declares, *"The words of the Lord are pure words; as silver tried in a furnace of earth, purified seven times."*

Therefore, when *Ephesians 4:23* tells us *"To be renewed in the spirit of your minds,"* this renewal must occur at the inner core of our being, which includes our motives, desires, attitudes, and thoughts. This is what it means to be born again. Everything about us needs to be made new when we come to Christ: our value system, our way of doing life, our way of acting towards others, our way of speaking, and our way of thinking. Everything must be made new!

The Holy Spirit brings about these changes in us as we renew our minds with the Holy Scriptures and then as we look for practical ways to implement the Word of God in our lives. Just as *Psalm 19:7* states in the literal translation, *"The Word of God is completely able to restore the soul to its original design."* How awesome that is! The Holy Scriptures through the inner working of the Holy Spirit can do in us what the world can never do. Each time we put into practice biblical ways of thinking and acting, God can transform us from glory to glory.

As we spend time in the Word of God, rightly dividing it, we will not be deceived. Just as a bank teller is trained to recognize counterfeit money by spending hours studying genuine bills, you will be able to recognize a counterfeit gospel. The lies of this world and the voice of the enemy will become more discernible the more you devote yourself to spending quality time reading and studying God's Word. As you allow the Holy Spirit to renew your mind you will begin to love, seek after, and value what God says are the greater things. Beloved, we are truly in a battle. (*Ephesians 6:12*)

Write out two specific prayers from the Word of God you can use to start renewing your mind.

Personal Application

Review Days 1 through 4 of this week's study and answer the following questions.

1. According to the scriptures we looked at in Day 2, are you responsible for your husband's sin? (Use scriptures to support your answer.)

2. In Day 3 we looked at what the Bible has to say about our bodies. How does this contradict what the world tells us as women?

3. What lies have you believed from this world about your sexuality?

4. Based on question 3, develop a plan to counteract those lies with the truth of God's Word.

5. Give practical ways for how you can begin to daily renew your mind with God's Word.

Week Four, Day 1, Monday

Dealing with Anger, Bitterness, & Resentment

A Personal Testimony

Often, we do not understand why our spouses may treat us in the way they do. Especially if you ask them to do something as they are watching a football game or possibly engaged in an activity in which you are trying to get his attention. It is in those moments when he may respond in an unchristlike manner to your request. As you wonder at his response, you might even react by saying to him, "What is your problem? I just asked you a simple question?" Meanwhile, the Holy Spirit responds back to you by whispering, *"No, what is YOUR problem that you have an attitude over how he just answered you?"* Have you ever had that happen to you? I have, in more ways than I would like to admit.

There were many times early on in my marriage when my husband would be snappy with me for no good reason (as I just described in the football game scenario). I couldn't figure out why when I would ask Jeff a personal question he would respond so harshly. At the same time, God was showing me that it wasn't all about Jeff's sin. He was interested in what was going on in my heart whenever Jeff reacted in this way. Each time he would do this, I would want to distance myself from him. Little by little we had built up a wall between us that seemed impenetrable. Likewise, we both were harboring a root of bitterness in our hearts towards one another.

A dear friend of mine once told me, "Bitterness is like the acid within your body which you want to spew on others; but before you get the chance to do so it will eat you alive." This deadly cancer is a malignancy of the soul as we are warned of in *Psalm 37:8, "Cease from anger, and forsake wrath; do not fret; it only causes harm."* Throughout the years of counseling, I have witnessed this truth in the lives of many women. Anger, bitterness, and resentment are like lethal venom that have the power to destroy both the physical body, as well as the individual's spiritual health. What is so scary about this toxin is addressed in *Proverbs 14:10, "The heart knows his own bitterness."* Why then would we hold onto a poisonous viper knowing it is causing us harm and has the power to kill us?

I found this to be true in my own life when Jeff was in unrepentant sin. This bitterness would rear its ugly head at church whenever I would talk to other women about my husband. Whenever they would ask me how things were going with my spouse I would spew this ugly venom, which Jesus said comes from the heart. *(Matthew 15:18-19)* I knew what I was doing but I really did not care. I was hurt. In all honesty, I wanted these ladies to despise my husband and what he was doing to me. The anger, bitterness, and resentment that came out of my mouth was like molten lava flowing from a volcano that had erupted. It was very destructive, destroying my spouse's reputation among these ladies and the testimony of Christ in me. As Jesus said in *Matthew 12:34-35,*

> *"For out of the abundance of the heart the mouth speaks. The good person out of the good treasure brings forth good, but the evil person out of his evil treasure brings forth evil."*

There were times when this deadly toxin would manifest itself, especially in the early years of our marriage. For example, there was a night Jeff called and told me he would be home late from work. I waited, and waited, and waited; Jeff never came home. I was so angry! I took all his clothes and threw them out of the fifth floor of our apartment building. I did not care what anyone thought about this crazy lady throwing his personal belongings out the window. Jeff knew when he came home and found his clothes strewn out on the hedges that he was in trouble. But he had a way of sweet-talking his way back into the home with beautiful bouquets of exotic flowers that always seemed to win my heart.

There was another time Jeff and I were home just talking. He had been drug-free for several months but out of the clear blue I turned around and told him, *"I hate you!"* Then I proceeded to punch him in the face. He was stunned. Neither of us had any idea where that came from. I thought all along I was dealing with the hurt in my heart, but my actions proved otherwise. God bless my husband, because he just held me in his arms and began to say, "Rose, let God remove the stone away from your heart." I broke down in tears.

I finally cried out, "God, I need you to help me get rid of this hostility from my heart." You see, the frightening thing about all of this was how subtle the bitterness had grown; just as a slithering snake can catch you off guard. I never realized what was happening until I responded in this way. Instead of dealing biblically with my emotions, I was stuffing them down, "sweeping them under the rug." I thought because I was a born-again Christian I should not acknowledge that I was struggling with these things because, "*I was a new creation in Christ.*" However, I did not understand as a believer there was a war going on in my own flesh and spirit. It was the same war my husband was fighting. Because of this contamination, I was allowing satan to eat up any love I had in my heart. If God had not granted me a spirit of repentance, the bitterness in my heart would have eventually ravaged and destroyed my marriage. The result of uncontrollable anger, bitterness, and resentment can only bring destruction into relationships. That is why in *Proverbs 4:23* we are told,

> *"Keep your heart with all vigilance, for from it flow the springs of life."*

I realized I too needed help. I wanted to learn how to conquer this sin so it would not rule and reign in me. I began to work on a Bible study my pastor's wife shared with me. Through the studies I began to see the sinfulness of my heart. The Holy Spirit showed me that I was sinning every time I verbally attacked my husband's character. I was not loving my neighbor as myself. When I was honest before the Lord, I acknowledged that I desired for Jeff to "feel" the hurt he had caused me since he had been treating me so horribly. Yes, I wanted Jeff to stop sinning against me. However, when he hurt me I felt justified in my anger toward him. Yet the scriptures showed me that by not dealing with my anger in the way God desired, I was bearing the works of the sinful nature in my marriage (*Galatians 5:19-21*). Even though I believed I had every right to be angry with Jeff, I discovered I did not have any of those rights when I looked at Jesus and what He had done for me on the cross. As I began to study the life of Jesus Christ, the Holy Spirit (through the Word of God) revealed to me how Jesus was sinned against. As I reflected on my dear Savior's life my heart began to soften towards my husband.

Consider for a moment what God allowed His Beloved Son to face while He lived here on earth. Jesus was treated unjustly *(Matthew 26:65-67)*, He was despised and rejected by men, a man of sorrows and acquainted with grief *(Isaiah 53:3-4)*. He was bruised for our sakes *(Isaiah 53:10)*. He was ridiculed and mocked *(Matthew 27:27-31)*, falsely accused *(John 7:20)*, misunderstood by the religious leaders *(John 15:24)*, suffered injustices *(Matthew 27:1)*, felt forsaken and abandoned by God *(Psalm 22:1-2)*, was hated by all men *(Mark 15: 11-15)*, and so much more. Yet, never once do we ever read in the Gospels that He responded with sinful anger. Amazing, isn't He? Each time I would, *"Consider*

79

Him who endured such hostility from sinners against Himself" (Hebrews 12:3), little by little, God was able to roll away the stone from my heart that was blocking the flow of His agape love towards my husband. As I surrendered my rights, by choosing not to hold onto Jeff's sins, God began to perform a miracle in me. He was setting my imprisoned heart free, which I was not aware of until this trial came into our marriage. God loved me too much to allow what I had stuffed in my heart all these years to remain there.

What about you, my dear sister? How have you responded to your husband? Do you feel justified in your anger towards him? Is there some stone that needs to be rolled away from your heart today? Ask the Holy Spirit to reveal to you anything you might be holding onto from the past or present. As God begins to show you specific things, I encourage you to lay them down one by one at the feet of Jesus. As you begin to release your husband to Christ in this way, God will begin to perform a miracle in you. Please use space provided below to write out what God has shown you.

Week Four, Day 2, Tuesday

The Danger of Holding onto Anger, Bitterness, & Resentment

Jesus said to His disciples on the Sermon the Mount,

> *"You have heard that it was said to those of old, 'You shall not murder, and whoever murders will be in danger of the judgment.' But I say to you whoever is angry with his brother shall be in danger of the judgment." (Matthew 5:21-22)*

In the story of Cain and Abel in *Genesis 4:1-16*, the Lord confronted Cain because he was extremely angry over his brother's offering. Abel brought the acceptable offering to God and received God's favor while He did not receive Cain's offering because it was the wrong way to approach His Holy Presence. As a result, Cain was angry, bitter, and resentful towards his brother. *"So, the Lord said to Cain, "Why are you angry? And why has your countenance fallen? If you do well, will you not be accepted? And if you do not do well, sin lies at the door. And its desire is for you, but you should rule over it."* Only

81

God knows the thoughts that repeatedly churned in Cain's mind because of his rejection. He also knew Cain's angry heart would ultimately lead him into murdering his brother if he did not deal with it in God's way. Although God's desire was for Cain to rule over his emotions, sadly, Cain did not heed God's warning. We see the ultimate fruit of his sin and lack of fear of God's judgment when he rose up and killed Abel.

1. Read *Ephesians 4:26-27, 29-31.* Look up the Greek definition for: (1) *bitterness, (2) wrath, (3) anger, (4) clamor, (5) evil speaking, and (6) malice* in a Strong's Concordance.

2. What happens when we hold onto anger, bitterness, and resentment *(verse 30)*?

3. Write out the Greek definition for *grieved.*

4. What does *Proverbs 21:19* say about a contentious and angry woman?

5. How does anger manifest itself in a person and in a relationship according to *Proverbs 25:23-24*?

6. What danger are we in when we hold onto anger according to *Proverbs 29:22?*

7. What does *Ecclesiastes 7:9* call someone who is harboring anger in their heart?

As you examined these scriptures, would you say the sin of bitterness is crouching at the door of your heart? If so, God's desire is that you would begin to master it, today.

Are you willing to allow the Holy Spirit to help you to mortify or to put to death the different sinful forms of anger that we read about in *Ephesians 4:29, 31,* and to put on *"being kind to one another, tenderhearted, forgiving one another, even as God in Christ forgave you?" (Ephesians 4:32)* If you will repent of your sinful responses, God will liberate your heart and begin the healing process in your relationship with your spouse.

Write out a prayer of repentance to the Lord in the space provided below.

But You Don't Know
What He Did to Me

There have been many times in counseling I have heard a wife say, "But it seems so unfair that I cannot cling to my anger, bitterness, or resentment against my husband." But as they begin to consider Jesus crying out from the cross of Calvary, "*Father, forgive them. For they know not what they do*" they realize "How can I justify my anger when nothing but agape love flowed from His heart at Calvary for me?" As *Romans 5:6* tells us,

> "*For when we were still without strength, in due time Christ died for the ungodly.*"

God blessed these precious women with the grace needed to let go of each offense they were holding onto towards their mate despite the number of times their spouse had sinned against them. Undeniably, this was not easy to do. However, God was looking at their hearts to see if they would be obedient to His Word and not allow themselves to wallow in self-pity.

As you read the following scriptures, allow the Holy Spirit to minister to your heart. Write out what He shows you.

1. *Matthew 26:47-56*

2. *Matthew 27:11-31*

3. *Mark 14:55-65*

4. *Mark 15:12-20*

5. *Luke 23:13-25, 34*

My dear friend, Jesus did all of this not only for you but for your husband also.

The apostle Paul wrote in *Romans 8:18,*

"For I consider that the sufferings of this present time are not worthy to be compared with the glory which shall be revealed in us."

Although God is calling you to suffer the loss of not holding onto your anger, bitterness, or resentment, there is a glory He desires to reveal in and through you as you choose to let go of each of your husband's offenses. The apostle Paul said, *"Christ in you is the hope of glory."* God's glory is an unconditional agape love which Jesus displayed to a lost and dying world from the cross. This "Christlike love" is what your family, children, friends, co-workers, and the lost and dying world needs to witness through your life in a real and tangible way.

Are you willing to allow Christ's love flow from your heart in this way? If so why don't you spend some time, at this moment, surrendering your heart to Him to walk in a manner worthy of what you have been called towards your husband starting today. *(Ephesians 4:1-3)*

Dealing Biblically with Anger, Bitterness, & Resentment

Today we will consider what Jesus told his disciples in *John 8:31-32,*

> *"If you abide in My word, you are My disciples indeed. And you shall know the truth and the truth shall make you free."*

My friend, there is a great freedom that awaits you today as you abide in the truth of God's Word and look for practical ways to implement it in your daily life.

1. Read *James 1:19-25.* Go through each verse and summarize the main points of this passage of scripture.

This passage translated in *The New Testament: An American Translation* by Edgar J. Goodspeed, states to "*Strip yourselves of everything that soils you, and of every evil growth.*" How do we do that? According to the same translation, it happens when we take the time "*To consider God's flawless law that makes men free.*" As we are obedient to God, the Holy Spirit can do this work of purification in our hearts. Our Heavenly Father desires for us to be liberated from every sinful attitude in our hearts that does not glorify Him. However, for this to happen, we must apply His Word by being doers of what He says even if our circumstances never change.

Read the following verses. Write out practical ways on how you can begin to deal with anger, bitterness, and resentment God's way.

2. *Proverbs 19:11*

3. *Matthew 5:43-48*

4. *Romans 12:17-21*

5. *1 Corinthians 13:4-8*

6. Read *Colossians 3:5-15*

Each time I read *Titus 2:11-14*, I am encouraged of the promise of His grace to help me whenever I choose to put off sinful practices.

> *"For the grace of God that brings salvation has appeared to all men, teaching us that, denying ungodliness and worldly lusts, we should live soberly, righteously and godly in the present age, looking for the blessed hope and glorious appearance of our great God and Savior Jesus Christ, who gave Himself for us, that He might redeem us from every lawless deed and purify for Himself His own special people, zealous for good works."*

Will you allow the Holy Spirit to do this in you as you purpose in your heart to respond biblically to any sinful forms of anger which God may have shown you this week? God's grace will be there to help you every step of the way. Be encouraged, my sister. You are not alone in this.

Week Four, Day 5, Friday
Personal Application

Review Days 1 through 4 of this week's study and answer the following questions.

1. What form of sinful anger are you harboring in your heart towards your husband?

2. How do you know? How does it manifest itself?

3. Do you feel you have a right to be angry with your mate? Why?

4. In Day 4 of our study, what must you do to show fruits of repentance towards your spouse?

5. Write out a plan of action that you can implement when you are tempted to be angry, bitter, or resentful toward your husband.

But How Many Times Do I Keep Forgiving Him?

A Personal Testimony

"Forgive my husband, AGAIN? But Jeff doesn't deserve to be forgiven! Do you know how many times I have forgiven him over and over, only for him to keep doing what he is doing? This just doesn't seem fair?" Countless times I have asked these exasperated questions of God and my Pastors when I turned to them for counsel while Jeff was still in his sin. In fact, I have heard these words from many Christian women over the years who proclaim to love God with all their hearts. However, I wonder if God is ever perplexed when He looks His children. We call ourselves followers of Christ, yet are we willing to walk in ongoing forgiveness towards those who transgress against us? Do we really believe what Jesus said in *Matthew 6:14*?

> *"For if you forgive men their trespasses, your heavenly Father will also forgive you. But if you do not forgive men their trespasses, neither will your Father forgive your trespasses."*

While this most definitely will be an intense mental and emotional challenge as we wrestle through this issue of forgiveness, God still requires it.

In this week's study we will look at Ephesians and many other passages of scripture that address this topic. What we will learn from them is God's will is that we, *'Forgive one another even as God 'in Christ' forgave you.'* For us to begin to walk in this kind of biblical forgiveness, we need to take a look at God's ongoing vertical forgiveness towards us.

When we look at the Greek definition of the word *forgive* in Matthew 6:14 (aphiemi) it means: *to let go, to give up a debt, to remit, to keep no longer and to abandon.* It is interesting that Jesus spoke these words to His disciples in the context of prayer. God's teaching on forgiveness is not a suggestion; rather, it is a requirement to approach His Holy throne room of grace through prayer. The Holy Spirit began to show me, *"If I regard iniquity in my heart, the Lord will not hear me."* (*Psalm 66:18*) I was kidding myself if I thought I could truly seek God while refusing to let go of an unforgiving attitude in my heart toward my husband. How unchristlike I was to keep a record of wrongs and to justify this sinful attitude in my heart towards my spouse. (This was especially true considering who God is.)

> *Ephesians 2:1-7 states, "And you He made alive, who were dead in trespasses and sins, in which you once walked according to the course of this world, according to the prince of the power of the*

air, the spirit who now works in the sons of disobedience among whom also we all once conducted ourselves in the lusts of the flesh, fulfilling the desires of the flesh and of the mind, and were by nature children of wrath, just as the others. BUT GOD, who is RICH IN MERCY, because of HIS GREAT LOVE with which HE LOVED US, even while we were dead in trespasses, made us alive together with Christ Jesus, that in the ages to come He might show THE EXCEEDING RICHES OF HIS GRACE, IN KINDNESS TOWARDS US IN CHRIST JESUS." (Emphasis added)

When I considered God's vertical forgiveness towards me, how could I be so stingy to not extend this same grace of horizontal forgiveness to my husband? Even though there were many times I would ask Jesus, *"Lord how many times shall my brother sin against me, and I forgive him? Up to seven times?* Jesus would say to me, *"I do not say to you* (Rose), *up to seven times, but up to seventy times seven (Matthew 18:21)."* In all honesty, these were not the words I wanted to hear. It seemed so much easier for me to hold onto my grudges and resentments.

As we look at this subject of forgiveness, Jesus told Peter to forgive up to seventy times seven. He was not saying when you get to four hundred and ninety times of forgiving someone, you no longer must extend them this grace. No. Jesus knew if we practice ongoing horizontal forgiveness towards others, eventually it will become a natural outflow of our heart to those who transgress against us. Whether that person comes to us and ask for forgiveness or not, our heart will be free from this trap which has its roots in many poisonous works of the flesh that subtly ensnare us (*Galatians 5:19-21*).

As I would reflect on what Jesus has done for me on the cross, the Holy Spirit began to search my heart and I realized my heart had grown callous over the years. Although I would frequently wrestle over what Jesus was saying to me in my heart and in my mind, deep down inside I knew that God was right and my sinful attitude towards my husband was wrong. Just as Peter tried to justify his unforgiving attitude toward his brother by asking Him if he was to forgive only up to seven times, I too was looking for an excuse not to forgive my spouse. I was afraid of being hurt again. Thankfully, the Lamb of God who takes away the sins of the world provided us an example to follow.

As I would walk through this ongoing mental and emotional struggle of forgiveness towards Jeff, the Holy Spirit would constantly remind me of God's vertical forgiveness towards me. It was during those times that I would see how I needed to repent of my unloving attitude towards my husband. The challenge then became this: Was I willing to walk in *1 Corinthians 13:4-8* towards Jeff even though he continued to sin against me?

> *"Love suffers long and is kind; love does not envy; love does not parade itself, is not puffed up; does not behave rudely, does not seek its own, is not*

provoked, thinks no evil; does not rejoice in inquiry, but rejoices in the truth; bears all things, believes all things, hopes all things, endures all things. Love never fails.

This love that we read about is what God expected me to live in and demonstrate towards my spouse, whether I felt he deserved it or not. God was testing my heart to see how I would respond in this situation *(Jeremiah 17:10)*. Regardless of how many times Jeff had sinned against me, as a follower of Christ, God expected me to walk in His biblical love and show horizontal forgiveness towards him. As the eyes of my heart opened to God's amazing love and grace in my life, this icy heart of mine began to melt.

Each time I struggled over this issue of forgiveness in my heart, I had to make a conscious choice to not dwell on my husband's offense in my mind. Instead of hitting the replay button, God wanted me to take my thoughts captive to Him. It was in those times, I had to learn how to apply these biblical truths that we just read in *1 Corinthians 13:4-8* whenever the enemy would stir up fiery accusatory darts over Jeff's offenses against me. As the Holy Spirit would gently remind me of God's vertical love and acceptance when I was at my worst back in October 12, 1984. My spiritual condition at that time is described in Ezekiel *16:6, 8-9,*

> *"When I passed by you and saw you struggling in your own blood, I said to you in your blood, 'Live!' ...I spread My wing over you and covered*

99

your nakedness. Yes, I swore an oath to you and entered into a covenant with you and you became Mine, says the Lord God. I washed you in water, yes, I thoroughly washed off your blood and I anointed you with oil…"

If God so loved me in this way, what right did I have to keep a record of wrongs towards Jeff by continually rehearsing them in my mind? Every time I would do this it would be as if the incident was happening again for the first time. It was just like picking a scab off of a wound, preventing it from healing completely. To protect an injury, a scab forms to keep out the bacteria and give the skin cells underneath a chance to heal. As I chose to nurse my unforgiving heart, I kept ripping off the healing scab of grace. Whenever I would do this, I would open the door to the accuser of the brethren. By giving him access to my heart and mind in this way, I would expose myself once again to the pain and the tormenting thoughts as I rehearsed my husband's offenses in my thinking. Many times, I would reopen the very sore that God was trying to heal by allowing the germs of an unforgiving attitude to re-infect my heart. Whenever we do this, we hinder God from bringing about the freedom that we need.

What about you, my friend? I know you are afraid of being hurt by your husband again, but can you recount how God 'in Christ' has loved and forgiven you? Take some time to think about God's ongoing vertical forgiveness towards you during your lifetime. If it helps, you can write them down in a journal, a notebook, or in the space below. When you are done, take that list before the Lord in prayer, and with thanksgiving in your heart, ask Him for His grace to help you to release your husband's offenses in the same way. As you do this, your heart will begin to open to the amazing wonder of God's love through Christ in a fresh new way.

God's Vertical Forgiveness Towards Us 'In Christ Jesus'

What a loving and merciful God that He would demonstrate His love towards mankind through His Beloved Son's death on the cross (*John 3:16*). Our dear Savior's heartfelt cry to the Father from Calvary is such a beautiful picture of our Abba Father's unconditional love and vertical forgiveness for you and me. This precious gift of salvation is truly more valuable than any other treasure here on earth.

1. Read *1 Peter 1:18-21* and *Isaiah 1:18*.

It is hard to fathom how just one drop of Jesus' sacred blood can wash away each one of our sins. In fact, in *Hebrews 9:22* we read, "*Without the shedding of blood there can be no remission of sin.*" In *verses 11-14,* we are told, "*The blood of bulls, goats and calves* (which was required as the high priest came into the temple in Jerusalem), *could not redeem us.*" However, Jesus Christ our Great High Priest has passed through the heavens and is right at this moment seated at the right hand of the

Father. He alone *"Can cleanse our conscious from dead works to serve the living God."* (*verse 14*) This is the good news of the Gospel. *"Christ is the Mediator of the new covenant."* (*Hebrews 9:15*) This new covenant promises us, *"No more shall every man teach his neighbor and every man his brother, saying 'Know the Lord,' for they all shall know Me, from the least of them to the greatest of them,"* says the Lord. *"For I will forgive their iniquity, and their sin I will remember no more."* How utterly lost we would be if He did not do this for us, my friend.

2. According to the Strong's Concordance, what does it mean when God says, *"their sin I will remember no more?"*

God has entered a blood covenant with us through the death of His Son. Once we repent and confess our sins He promises *"not to remember"* (or not to act on), as well as, *"not to mention by bringing them to mind"* (or to refrain from acting upon) again.

Please take a moment to reflect on *Isaiah 53*. As you do, prayerfully consider each verse of God's vertical forgiveness towards you. As you, *"Consider Him who endured such hostility from sinners against Himself... "* realizing, *"you have not yet resisted to bloodshed"* in your *"striving against sin... " (Hebrews 12:3-4),* you will be able to offer horizontal forgiveness towards your husband. Remember God's grace will be available to you as you are obedient in submitting yourself to the Holy Spirit and Word of God in this way. *(Titus 2:11-14)*

Read through the following passages of scripture. What else do you discover about God's vertical forgiveness?

3. *Isaiah 43:25 and 44:22*

4. *Jeremiah 33:8*

5. *Psalm 32:1-2; Psalm 103:12; Psalm 130:3-4*

6. *Micah 7:18-19*

7. *Colossians 2:13*

8. *1 John 1:9*

My dear sister, God has so loved us and our husbands in this way. Although we remember the sins committed against us, God has called us in *John 15:12* to love just as He loves and to forgive as He has forgiven us, '*in Christ.*' As you choose to meditate often on God's ongoing vertical forgiveness in your life, His grace will be there to help you '*to not mention or to recall*' to mind your spouse's sin. Each time you choose not to keep a record of wrongs or not to talk to others about his offense, God's love is being perfected in you. (See *1 John 4:12).*

Why don't you write out a commitment statement, sign and date it as a reminder to forgive your spouse just as God '*in Christ*' has forgiven you? Then, review it often whenever you are tempted to bring up his sin against you whether verbally or mentally.

But I'm Not God

It can be a real challenge to see how unlike the Father we are in this area of biblical forgiveness. The human heart is so prone to hold onto offenses and repeatedly replay them in our minds. Sometimes we can even feel justified in harboring our sin, especially if our offender never comes to us and asks if we would forgive them. But let us consider *Matthew 18:21-35* for a moment.

Read through *Matthew 18:21-35* and answer the following questions.

1. According to Jesus, what is the kingdom of heaven like in *verse 23*?

2. What happened to the servant who couldn't settle his account of ten thousand talents in *verse 25*?

3. What did that servant do before his master in *verse 26*?

4. How did his master respond to his request in *verse 27*?

5. What then did that servant do to a fellow servant who owed him a hundred denarii in *verse 28?*

6. In *verse 29*, how did his fellow servant respond to the one who was shown compassion and forgiveness?

7. How did the one who had received mercy respond to this servant in *verse 30*?

8. How did the master respond when he heard how this fellow servant put him in prison and demanded that he pay his debt in full according to *verses 31-34?*

9. What did Jesus say in *verse 35?*

The amazing aspect of this parable is when you look at the equivalent of ten thousand talents in our modern currency. Ten thousand talents would be around four to five million dollars today, while a hundred denarii would be about thirty-two thousand dollars. I do not know about you, but I have been forgiven ten thousand talents. It is a debt I can never repay.

Beloved, even though it can be a challenge to walk in this kind of biblical forgiveness towards those who have transgressed against us, God still requires it. He has a right to ask this from His children because of how He has forgiven us. This parable so beautifully illustrates the enormity of true forgiveness. Refusing to offer the same horizontal forgiveness towards others opens us up to the world of darkness in which satan reigns.

10. Look up *Ephesians 4:26-27* in the Amplified Bible. Write out what is stated.

11. What does *1 John 4:20-21* say about us when we do not walk in love towards our brother?

My friend, when we choose to walk in biblical forgiveness towards another it does not mean we condone that person's behavior. Rather we are making a conscious decision, in our heart, to not let their offense control us. Choosing to walk in forgiveness is freeing!

The Need to Live in Ongoing Horizontal Forgiveness

In *Genesis chapters 25, 27, and 33,* we have the life history of two brothers, Esau and Jacob. Esau was Isaac's first-born son who, according to Jewish tradition, was to be consecrated for God's service. However, in *Genesis 25*, Jacob is described as envious of his brother's birthright.

Likewise, Esau despised his heritage so much that he sold it to Jacob for a bowl of stew. As their father Isaac lay dying, his eyesight had faded and he could not see clearly. Jacob took advantage of the situation and deceived his father by making him think he was Esau so that he could receive his father's blessing. Later, we read in *Genesis chapter 27* that when Esau found out his brother had deceived his dad, he was furious. However, by the time we get to *Genesis 33,* we see that something had changed in Esau's heart towards Jacob.

When word came to Esau that his brother was approaching with all his family members, Esau ran to meet Jacob; he hugged, and kissed him. Esau's display of forgiveness and mercy toward Jacob is an example for us to follow. Although it 'seemed' Esau had every right to hold on to an unforgiving attitude in his heart toward his brother Jacob, his actions proved otherwise.

In the *Gospel of Luke 17:1*, Jesus told His disciples,

"It is impossible that no offenses should come."

The context of this passage has to do with how to deal with a brother who sins against us. Moreover, in *verses 3 through 4,* Jesus said,

"Take heed to yourselves. If your brother sins against you, rebuke him; and if he repents, forgive him. And if he sins against you seven time in a day, and seven times in a day returns to you, saying, 'I repent' you shall forgive him."

As we see in this portion of scripture, Jesus is serious about this issue of extending ongoing horizontal forgiveness towards those who continue to repeat the same sin against us.

Read the following scriptures and then write out practical ways we can live in continual ongoing forgiveness towards others.

1. *Matthew 5:23-24*

2. *Matthew 6:12-15; Luke 11:4*

3. *Mark 11:25-26*

4. *2 Corinthians 2:3-11*

5. *Ephesians 4:32*

6. *Colossians 3:13*

As we read *2 Corinthians 2:14, 15*, the apostle Paul stated,

> *"Now thanks be to God, who always leads us in triumph in Christ, and through us diffuses the fragrance of His knowledge in every place. For we are to God the fragrance of Christ among those who are being saved and among those who are perishing."*

Beloved, this is so true when we choose to walk in what Jesus told His disciples in *Luke 17:1*. Through our lives, Christ can display His glory to a lost and dying world that needs to know the message of the Cross (His vertical and horizontal forgiveness), in a very real and tangible way. Will you allow Him to do this in your heart today? If so, spend some time in prayer.

Week Five, Day 5, Friday

Personal Application

Review Days 1 through 4 of this week's study and answer the following questions.

1. Review Day 2 of your homework. Write out how God has vertically forgiven you 'in Christ'?

2. Based on the parable Jesus told of the unjust servant in Day 3, are there specific things you are holding onto towards your husband? If so, write them out.

3. How do you feel that your husband "owes you" or deserves to be punished in a certain way?

4. How have you been seeking revenge or justifying your sinful attitude?

5. What must you do to walk in biblical forgiveness towards your husband based on Day 4?

Overcoming Fear, Worry, & Anxiety Over the Unknown

A Personal Testimony

As Jeff and I were endeavoring to move forward in his striving against sin, I had to learn to find rest in God in a greater way. This became real to me as I was dealing with the fear of what the future held for us as a couple. This was mercifully pointed out to me while Jeff and I were on an excursion with a friend of his. I remember expressing these emotions to this friend related to things I could not control about my husband. After he listened to the words coming out of my heart, he said to me, "You need God to break you free from the bondage of fear, worry, and anxiety you are in."

I remember when he said this it was like a wake-up call. At that moment I realized my focus was in the wrong place and person. As I pondered his words, I noticed whenever I focused on the waves and the wind of the unknown which could potentially blow into my marriage, it was as if I would sink into a sea of shark-infested waters that would eat me up inside. As I began to sink under this wave of fluctuating emotions, I cried out

117

to our Savior to save me just as He did for Peter on the Sea of Galilee in *Matthew 14:22-33*. There were many times when Jesus rebuked me and said, *"Why are you so fearful, O you of little faith?" (Matthew 8:26)* Do you not realize who *I AM* by now?

Shortly after this incident, the Lord put a precious lady in my life who I could talk to about my inner struggles. This dear saint spent an hour talking and praying with me. It was such a wonderful time that I will always cherish in my heart. As I shared my anxieties with her, she asked me a simple question, "Why are you wasting your time worrying about things you have no control over?" She then said, "Instead of fretting over the unforeseen future, you need to get your eyes on the One who is Faithful."

What I had come to see about my heart was that the more my eyes were fixed on Jeff, what he was or was not doing biblically, the more I was consumed with these emotions. However, as I fixed my eyes on Jesus, who is at this very moment seated at the right hand of the Father interceding on my behalf, my heart was flooded with great peace. Living in the reality, God saw all things and, similar to how He revealed this to Hagar in *Genesis 16:11-13*, He provided a great calmness of heart, even though we still faced an unknown future. I needed to learn how to practice and rest in what the Psalmist wrote in *Psalm 121,* whenever I was struggling with my feelings:

> *"I will lift up your eyes to the hills from whence comes my help? My help comes from the Lord,*

who made heaven and earth. He will not allow your foot to be moved; He who keeps you will not slumber, Behold, He who keeps Israel shall neither slumber nor sleep. The Lord is your keeper; the Lord is your shade at your right hand. The sun shall not strike you by day, nor the moon by night. The Lord shall preserve you from all evil; He shall preserve your soul. The Lord shall preserve your going out and your coming in from this time forth and even forevermore."

As I continued to meditate on Peter's encounter with Jesus on the Sea of Galilee, I had to frequently remind myself that He is Lord over the winds and waves of the sea just as *Nahum 1:3-4* states,

"The Lord has His way in the whirlwind and in the storm, and the clouds are the dust of His feet. He rebukes the sea and makes it dry and dries up all the rivers."

God is Sovereign. He is in absolute control of every whirlwind, storm cloud, and the raging sea that may come into my life. Since He revealed this knowledge of Himself to me, I realize I must not waste valuable time being fearful, worried, or anxious about anything. Trials are an opportunity for God to train us to look at Him more, through His Word, rather than looking at the mountains and the giants that lay before us. As *Isaiah 26:3-4* states,

"You will keep him in perfect peace, whose mind is stayed on You, because he trusts in You. Trust

in the Lord forever, for in YAH, the Lord, is everlasting strength."

These two passages of scripture became a lifeline to me I needed to rest in whenever these feelings rose up in my heart and in my thinking.

I was given an assignment to look up all the scripture verses that speak of God's faithfulness and sovereignty. Little did I know how freeing this counsel would be to me in the years to come in other areas of my life. Through my struggle against fear, worry, and anxiety, the Holy Spirit began to teach me the need to live in *Philippians 4:6, 8-9.*

With every trial I faced I saw how *the Lord is near* and I could *rejoice in* this truth whenever I was tempted to become anxious about anything. I also learned how to *pray about everything* instead of sitting around thinking about all the "what-ifs". Likewise, I had to habitually practice *biblical thinking,* by meditating on *"whatever things are noble, whatever things are just, whatever things are pure, whatever things are lovely, whatever things are of a good report, if there is anything that is virtuous and praiseworthy" (Philippians 4:8-9)* each time a situation aroused my emotions.

As the Holy Spirit helped me to practice being a doer of God's Word, *the God of peace* was with me, just as He promised. In the same way, *2 Timothy 1:7* stated, *"For God had not given you a spirit of fear but of power, love and sound mind"* started to become my reality.

Through the many trials that Jeff and I have faced over the past 27 years of being married, I continue to learn how to put these scriptures into practice, so I will not be ruled by my feelings.

Jesus told his disciples in *John 16:33,*

"These things I have spoken to you, that 'in Me' you may have peace. In the world you will have tribulation; but be of good cheer, I have overcome the world."

No matter what the future holds for any of us, if we are 'abiding in Christ' we will have His peace ruling and reigning in our hearts. However, if we allow our hearts to focus on things which are totally out of our control, then we will reap the symptoms of fear, worry, and anxiety in our bodies. Why not allow your current situation to serve as an opportunity for you to meditate on God's faithfulness and sovereignty? You don't have to waste another precious moment looking at the 'what if's' that could potentially blow into your life. God has proven through His Word that He is faithful and true to everything He says about Himself! Through each and every hardships we face in life, it is His desire that the *"Word of God would dwell in us richly in all wisdom."* *(Colossians 3:16)*

To prepare your heart for this week's Bible study you might want to pray through or sing *Psalm 139:23-24.* Ask the Holy Spirit to, *"Search me, O God, and know my heart; try me, and know my anxieties; and see if there is*

121

any wicked way in me, and lead in the way everlasting." Be willing to take an honest look at what you really believe about God when trials come into your marriage. What are you placing your trust in during those times? Is it in the wrong thing or in the wrong direction? The Holy Spirit will bring correction into your life and begin to train you in biblical living and thinking if you allow Him to do so. God can set you free from the chains of fear, worry, and anxiety that imprison you on the inside. As you continually focus on every aspect of who God is and how He is in control of everything that happens, you will begin to experience, *"The peace of God which surpasses all understanding." (Philippians 4:9)*

Where is My Trust?

It can be extremely difficult for a wife to trust again when her marriage has been built on a foundation of lies. Tormenting thoughts may plague her mind with all the facts of what her husband has done and all the deception that has occurred as he has attempted to cover up his sin throughout the years. She may wonder, "Can I ever let down my guard and put my trust in my spouse again?" That is a question she may ponder over and over again in her mind. At other times, she may even wrestle with, "How can I trust God will not allow me to go through this again?"

If a wife continues to allow her lack of trust to rule and reign in her heart, she will become suspicious of every little thing her mate does. As she allows these emotions to fester in her heart, what she is basically saying is, "God you are neither sovereign nor are you good; therefore; I must take matters into my own hands." This wife then becomes trapped in a vicious cycle of trying to keep her husband under her surveillance, which will eventually lead her into bondage. I cannot tell you how many times I have seen this in counseling. But as we consider these things, read the following scriptures and note what they say about where our trust should or shouldn't be.

1. *2 Samuel 22:2-20*

2. *Proverbs 3:5-6*

3. *Proverbs 3:25-26*

4. *Jeremiah 17:5-8*

5. *Isaiah 31:10*

My friend, if our trust is in the wrong thing, the result will be worry, fear, and anxiety. Each time we are fearful of what man might do to us, according to *Matthew 10:28-31* and *Luke 12:4-5,* we sin. Our trust must be in the Lord and in Him alone. As we grow in our knowledge of God, we learn we don't have to monitor every move our husband's make. Ladies, God is faithful. He will bring into the light the things which are hidden in secret *(Luke 8:17; Mark 4:22)*.

We see this in the life of Rachel when she tried to hide the household idols from Jacob that she stole from her father, Laban *(see Genesis 31)*. Then there is Achan when he pillaged Jericho and thought he could hide what he had done from Joshua *(Joshua 7)*. Likewise, David when he sinned with Bathsheba and tried to cover up his sin for one full year. But God loved him too much to allow him to stay in his deception, so he sent Nathan the prophet to confront him *(2 Samuel 12)*.

What I have seen firsthand over the years in ministry reflected in what we read in *Numbers 32:23*, which also serves as a warning to us, "...*be sure your sin will find you out*!" There are so many examples of this throughout the scriptures. Since God can be trusted in this way, rather than being consumed with what your spouse might do to you again, won't you allow Your Heavenly Father to bring you into a greater place of resting in Him? If so, spend some time talking to God about your study for today.

Trusting in My Own Self-Efforts

Throughout the years, I have witnessed numerous wives get extremely frustrated in their futile attempts to prevent their husband from sinning. Instead of her working out her own salvation with fear and trembling *(Philippians 2:12)*, she frantically tries to work out her husband's salvation by trusting in her own self efforts to save and transform him. This tactic will not yield any lasting fruit in his life. Moreover, the more she continues to engage in this exhausting behavior, the farther she will plummet into a downward spiral of an idolatrous obsession with her husband.

Let us take a moment to read *Genesis 3:16* to learn about the heart motive that drives us to do this. Look up the Hebrew word in the Strong's Concordance for *desire* and *rule* to see if we can answer that question.

1. What do you learn from these two definitions?

126

When we worry or fret about a situation, the root of those feelings come from a desire 'to be in control.' Although, it can be scary to completely release our husbands to God by laying them down on the altar, the result of our refusal to do this will be fear, worry, and anxiety. So then, the longer we delay in submitting to God when He is putting His finger on our idol, the less likely we will have no rest or peace. Rest and peace will come when we are completely obedient to Him. It is not until we raise the white flag in surrender, choosing to release our spouse in this way, that we will begin to experience freedom from these emotions that so easily ensnare us. As we take this step of faith and relinquish our trust in our own self efforts,

> *"God is able to do exceedingly and abundantly above all that we ask or think, according to the power that works in us" (Ephesians 3:20)* in our husbands. As it is God, through His Holy Spirit, *"who works in us to will and to do for His good pleasure." (Philippians 2:13)*

How then can a wife live a surrendered life, in this way, in order not to fall back into this vicious cycle?

a) First, she must repent of trusting in her own self efforts. She cannot bring about a true godly sorrow in her husband. That is something that only God can do through the conviction of the Holy Spirit *(2 Timothy 2:24-26).*

b) Second, she must learn how to put off the desire to rule her husband's behavior by putting on daily prayer where she surrenders her husband to God. (Look up Bible passages that apply to your situation. What are some scripture verses that you can pray on behalf of your husband? Write them out in the space provided.)

c) Third, she must learn to rest in the Lord as she waits for God to intervene on her husband's behalf. (List practical ways you can begin to enter into His rest as you are waiting on God's timing.)

Week Six, Day 4, Thursday

You Can Put
Your Trust in God

The more we allow God to mature us in our faith, through the various trials we face in our marriage, the more we learn we can put our trust in Him always. Look up the following verses and fill in the blank.

Genesis 15:1   God is my _____

Isaiah 54:4-5   God is my _____

Psalm 18:2   God is my _____

Psalm 19:14   God is my _____

Psalm 32:7   God is my _____

Psalm 42:11   God is my _____

Psalm 144:2　　　　　　　God is my _____

John 20:17b　　　　　　　God is my _____

2 Corinthians 1:13　　　　God is my _____

Romans 15:13　　　　　　God is my _____

Revelation 19:11　　　　　God is my _____

Whatever situation you find yourself in today, you can totally rely on your Abba Father. God is Omniscient, Omnipresent, Omnipotent, and Sovereign; He already knows all the events that are going to take place in our lifetimes. He is not surprised by any of them. Since this is true, my friend, you need not be fearful, worried, or anxious about anything. Just as *1 Peter 5:7* encourages us, you can *"Cast all your cares on Him, for He cares for you."* Why don't you spend some time doing this today? He really does care for you. Rest in that reality.

Personal Application

Review Days 1 through 4 of this week's study and answer the following questions.

1. Do you feel you can ever trust your husband again? Why or why not?

2. What are some fears that you have about your spouse?

3. According to the scriptures on Day 2, do you trust the Lord in the way the Bible admonishes us to? Why or why not?

4. How have you tried to control your husband?

5. List 5 practical ways you can begin to put your trust in the Lord.

What Value Can there be In Persevering?

A Personal Testimony

During the first three years of my marriage, I witnessed my husband trying so hard to not give into his sin. But, it was only a matter of time before he would digress just as the Bible describes, "*as a dog returns to his own vomit.*" *(Proverbs 26:11)* This was so heartbreaking for me to watch. It seemed as if this trial had become an insurmountable mountain standing in the way of us moving forward in our relationship with each other. There were many times I could not see what value there was in persevering? However, what we were learning through each defeat was, *"For a righteous man may fall seven times but he will rise again." (Proverbs 24:16)* As we were walking through this process of progressive sanctification, Jeff and I realized setbacks were normal. Even though Jeff had not experienced total freedom from his sin yet, he was learning how not to live out his Christian walk in his own ability. Through each failure, my husband would see his need to rely on the Holy Spirit and the importance of patterning his life according to God's Word in his heart. While all we had ever known was defeat, nevertheless, God would use these trials to purify and sanctify our hearts in a greater way.

As Jeff would go through different programs I would wonder, "How long is this going to last?" I really questioned if I could trust what God had done in my spouse after he finished Pure Life Ministries' residential program. Was I setting myself up for another disappointment?

After Jeff had graduated the program, we were employed by Pure Life Ministries for twenty-two years. There came a time when he had to take care of an errand for the ministry. I was busy with counseling, so I was unable to accompany him. Back then there were no cell phones as we have today, so I had no way of communicating with him while he was gone. When Jeff took longer than I thought he should have, immediately my old way of thinking began to kick in. I thought, "Where is he? Why is he taking so long? Why haven't I heard from him?" My mind was bombarded with the "what if's."

By the time Jeff returned I responded as if he had done something wrong. In Jeff's frustration at what he just went through, he responded to me sharply by saying, "What is wrong with you?" In my mind Jeff was guilty before I heard all the facts. The Bible speaks about this type of reaction in *Proverbs 18:13, "He who answers a matter before he hears it, it is folly and shame to him."* As Jeff began to share what had happened I could feel myself sinking lower and lower in my heart. I realized how wrong

I was to pronounce him guilty as charged before I heard all the evidence. The cause for his delay was due to a bad accident on the interstate. The traffic was at a total stand still for about an hour or so. Since there was no way of communicating with one another, he could not let me know. He was unable to get off the freeway because it was at a gridlock. Jeff knew I would be worried about him, so he was praying for me while he was waiting for the wreckage to be cleared.

I could tell Jeff was speaking the truth from the years of experience I had listened to him lying to me. There was a sincerity and honesty in his eyes I had never seen before. Jeff was finally becoming a new creation in Christ by living in the light with me and his spiritual leaders, which was something he had not done in the past. The more I saw my husband opening his heart to me by being vulnerable about his inner struggles, the more God showed me 'I could trust the work He had done in my husband.' Just as *1 John 1:5-10* states,

> *"This is the message which we have heard from Him and declare to you, that God is light and in Him is no darkness at all. If we say that we have fellowship with Him, and walk in darkness, we lie and do not practice the truth. But if we walk in the light as He is in the light, we have fellowship with one another, and the blood of Jesus Christ His Son cleanses us from all sin. If we say that we have no sin, we deceive ourselves, and the truth is not in us. If we confess our sins, He is faithful and just to forgive our sins and to cleanse us from all*

unrighteousness. If we say that we have not sinned, we make Him a liar, and His word is not in us."

These were the spiritual principles my husband was living in with me, before God, and with others. I am so thankful God gave me the grace to persevere through this trial to see this fruit of repentance in my husband's life. God had indeed done a work in Jeff's heart after all the years of waiting upon the Lord to set him free. Although there were many times I wanted to throw in the towel, the Holy Spirit kept reminding me of *Galatians 6:9,*

> *"Let us not grow weary while doing good, for in due season we shall reap if we do not lose heart."*

Persevering through these trials together was much like running a marathon race. On May 4th, 1991 when we said, "I do," we took off for our honeymoon in a sprint and with much excitement. However, after we returned and the dust began to settle, there were many mental, physical, and spiritual challenges we had to face about ourselves. Just as in a race, both of us would get tired along the way as runners do when they sprint around a track. At times, we fell, but we continued to get back up so that we could reach the finish line. Occasionally, we had doubts as to, "Why are we even doing this?" Every so often, we struggled in our faith; could God get us across the finish line? From time to time, when we faced all the hurdles that lay before us we thought, "I can't do this anymore." Instead of encouraging and praising my husband, I wanted to just resign from his cheerleading squad. But the apostle Paul told the church in Corinth,

> *"Do you not know that those who run in a race all run, but one received the prize? Run in such a way that you may obtain it. And everyone who competes for the prize is temperate in all things. Now they do it to obtain a perishable crown, but we for an imperishable crown. Therefore, I run thus: not with uncertainly. Thus, I fight: not as one who beats the air. But I discipline my body and bring it to subjection, lest, when I have preached to others, I myself should become disqualified. (1 Corinthians 9:24-27)*

That is what this race was all about. We had enlisted to run in this contest and it was physically and spiritually taxing. However, God desired to bring us to the place where we would pass the baton to Jesus, who alone could help us to finish out this course. Through all the failures and setbacks, we were learning what Paul told the church in Corinth, *"to discipline our bodies"* by bringing them into subjection to the Holy Spirit so that He could bring forth a testimony in which God could be glorified.

I understand, my sister, that you may be tired of the fight. At times, you might even want to throw in the towel. However, there is much value in persevering. At the end of your course, Jesus will be there waiting for you with arms wide open. May He continue to cheer you on and encourage your heart to preserve. If you have fallen in defeat, get back up and do not look back. Now is not the time to quit; keep going! You may be very close to the finish line. Keep your gaze fixed on the Prize; Jesus our triumphant King who has overcome the world, the flesh, and the devil. He will give you the grace and the strength to persevere in your final lap. He is more than able to get you across the finish line. May that be your testimony, one day.

In the space provided, tell of a time when you were tempted to give up.

Not Growing Weary

As we read in yesterday's assignment if we are true disciples of Christ, we have been enlisted to run in God's spiritual race that is set before us. Just as in a 5k marathon, where there are those who would cheer us on to the finish line, *Hebrews 12:1-3* tells us,

> *"Therefore we also, since we are surrounded by so great a cloud of witnesses, let us lay aside every weight, and the sin which so easily ensnares us, and let us run with endurance the race that is set before us, looking unto Jesus, the author and finisher of our faith, who for the joy that was set before Him endured the cross, despising the shame, and has sat down at the right hand of the throne of God. For consider Him who endured such hostility from sinners against Himself, lest you become weary and discouraged in your souls."*

There have been many times I have worked with a wife who has grown weary and discouraged while her husband is trying to *lay aside every weight and the sin which so easily ensnares* him. Usually what this wife would express to me is, "It seems as if with every step we take forward we take two steps back with every defeat."

1. However, according to *Hebrews 12:1-3,* what are we encouraged to do when we are discouraged?

2. Please read through the following Psalms: *Psalm 20:7; Psalm 63:6; Psalm 77:10-12; Psalm 92:1-2; Psalm 96:1-2;* and *Psalm 145:1-7.*

3. Based on these scripture verses, write out practical things you can do when you are discouraged or have grown weary.

It is normal to grow weary as we wait upon the Lord to bring forth the manifest presence of the Holy Spirit in our husband's life. But, we should consider the words David penned in *Psalm 27:14* to *"Wait upon the Lord;"* be *"of good courage,"* and God *"shall strengthen your hearts."* Isn't it interesting David repeated, *"Wait upon the Lord"* at the end of that scripture verse? This Hebrew word for *wait* is, with an expectancy that God will respond at the appointed time in answer to our prayers.

4. Read *Galatians chapter 6.*

This principle of sowing and reaping we read about in this chapter, reminds us of a farmer who plants a tiny seed into the ground and waits to harvest his produce 'at the appointed time.'

5. According to *James 5:7-11,* how we are to wait for a fruitful harvest to come forth?

My friend, as your husband continues to seek God daily while yielding his heart to Christ Lordship in his life, eventually the fruit of the Holy Spirit will come forth (*Galatians 5:22*).

May I encourage you to continue to wait prayerfully and patiently upon the Lord. God is able to do in your husband what you think is impossible. The Holy Spirit will bring forth the fruit of the Spirit in your spouse's life as he surrenders moment by moment to God in his heart, in his will and in his desires. It is my pray for you today that you will allow God to strengthen your heart through His Word as you are in this season of waiting upon Him.

Holding onto Faith During the Battle

In the Book of Hebrews, we have a simple definition of what faith is,

> *"Now faith is the substance of things hoped for, the evidence of things not seen." (Hebrews 11:1)*

Although, *"No one has seen God at any time; the Only Begotten Son Who is in the bosom of the Father, He has declared Him to us" (John 1:8)*. The disciples had this first-hand knowledge for they had witnessed Jesus' life here on earth, as well as, His death, resurrection, and ascension into heaven. When the apostle John was exiled on the island of Patmos because of the Word of God and for the testimony of Jesus Christ (*Revelation 1:9*), Jesus revealed Himself to John,

> *"As the faithful witness, the firstborn from the dead" (Revelation 1:5), "the Alpha and the Omega, the Beginning and the End, who is, who was and who is to come, the Almighty." (Revelation 1:8), "He is He who lives, was dead,*

who is alive forevermore, and has the keys of Hades and Death." (Revelation 1:18)

My friend, we do not have faith in something that is a vapor or a mist. No, Christ is alive forevermore and He is the substance of our faith *(1 Corinthians 15:3-8)*. You can have great confidence in our Mighty God and Wonderful Savior who, at this very moment, oversees everything that is going on in your marriage. Our Great Savior,

"Is the brightness of our Father's glory, the expressed image of His person, who upholds all things by the word of His power." (Hebrews 1:3)

In *Romans 8:34,* the apostle Paul wrote,

"Christ is now at the right hand of God, who also makes intercession for us."

Did you ever wonder what Jesus could be praying for you? Is it possible that your faith would not fail amid all you are facing? As you read the following scripture verses look at how the substance of our faith is described.

1. *Amos 5:27*

2. *Deuteronomy 10:17-18*

3. *Exodus 3:14*

4. *Psalm 24:7-10*

5. *Isaiah 9:6*

Beloved, no matter how difficult your situation, continue to hold onto Jesus who is the substance of your faith. Even though you might be feeling battle fatigued, Jesus told us in *Luke 18:1, "Men should always pray and not give up."* He hears you, just as God heard the children of Israel's groaning and remembered His covenant with them while they were in bondage (*Exodus 2:23-24)*. Their deliverance came when His people least expected it. God is still able to part the Red Sea, bring living waters out of a rock, feed His people with manna from heaven, raise the dead, heal the sick, give sight to the blind, bring the demonic back into his right frame of mind, multiply the fish and the loaves and still have extra left over.

Why don't you spend today meditating on the glorious splendor of His majesty and on His wonderful works? Find someone to who you can speak of His awesome deeds. Declare His greatness and goodness to every person God puts in your pathway today. The next time you attend a worship service, sing of His righteousness with all your might, just as *Psalm 145:5* encourages us to do. Let faith arise in your heart in the midst of the battle you are facing.

Becoming Your Husband's Helpmate

Have you ever taken time to reflect on what Adam and Eve's marriage relationship was like before the Fall in the Garden of Eden? *(Genesis 2 and 3)*

- The fellowship they had with God and each other
- How God created them to be one for life
- The perfect unity they walked in with their Creator and with one another

The marriage they had is hard to imagine because all we have known in this world is opposite of what they had. However, when God created Eve He said, "*it is not good for man to be alone. I will create a helper comparable for him.*" (*Genesis 2:18*)

1. Look up the Hebrew word in the Strong's Concordance for *helper*, which is *ezer*. Write out its definition.

My friend, God has created you to *complete, complement, correspond to, fit perfectly and adapt to* your husband. That is amazing, isn't it? But how does this all play out in your marriage? As you read the following scriptures, write out specific ways you can become your husband's helpmate.

2. *Proverbs 12:4*

3. *Proverbs 14:1*

4. *Proverbs 31:10-31*

5. *Ephesians 5:33*

6. *1 Corinthians 7:4-6*

7. *1 Corinthians 11:3*

8. *1 Peter 3:1-6*

9. *Titus 2:3-5*

Week Seven, Day 5, Friday

Personal Application

Review Days 1 through 4 of this week's study and answer the following questions.

1. Describe a time when you felt like giving up during this battle?

2. How have you grown weary or discouraged? (How do you know?)

3. What can you do to turn that around according to Day 2?

4. According to Day 3, how can you hold faith for your spouse while you are waiting upon the Lord?

5. What areas do you need to work on for you to become a suitable helper for your husband? (Commit these areas to prayer.)

Weeping Endures For a Night, but Joy Comes in the Morning

A Personal Testimony

As we come to our last week of this study, I am reminded of when Jeff and I recited our wedding vows and how I came into this marriage with an earthly perspective. My reason for marrying my husband was to find true happiness. I wanted his friendship and companionship as we walked through this life together. I looked to him for my financial security and desired for him to make me feel loved and appreciated. On that glorious day, I really believed we would live happily ever after. However, God had an eternal purpose in mind when we said, "I do." So, when the trials of life immediately came into our marriage God reminded me of the words that were penned by a man who had faced far greater afflictions than we ever will; the apostle Paul. Paul said this of trials,

> *"For our light affliction, which is but for a moment, is working for us a far more exceeding*

and eternal weight of glory, while we do not look at the things which are seen, but at the things which are not seen. For the things which are seen are temporary, but the things which are not seen are eternal." (2 Corinthians 4:17-18)

Through every heartache, disappointment, and unmet expectation, I saw God desiring to draw the two of us to Himself because He had eternity on His mind. Immediately, I began to see that I needed His perspective during all we were facing if I was to experience the biblical joy that the apostle James wrote about in *James 1:2-4,*

> *"To count it all joy when you fall into various trials, knowing that the testing of your faith produces patience. But let patience have its perfect work, that you may be perfect and complete, lacking nothing."*

The last thing I wanted to do was to 'count this as all joy.' In fact, there were many times when I would murmur, whine, and complain to God for allowing these things to come into our lives. Through this affliction, God was showing me that I had a choice to make. I could choose to be a disgruntled sour puss through these afflictions, allowing my heart to grow hard and bitter, or I could do what the apostle Paul wrote in *1 Thessalonians 5:18,*

> *"In everything give thanks; for this is the will of God in Christ Jesus for you."*

My sinful attitude revealed that I needed to thank God for allowing this trial to come early on in my marriage because He was using it to '*work an eternal weight of glory*' in me.

One of the ways I began to *give thanks* was by writing an ongoing gratitude list in a notebook on which I would frequently reflect. As I reviewed my journal, I rehearsed the many blessings of the trials we faced, which reassured me that all of this was not in vain. Even though there were many times of weeping as we were walking through this valley, I began to relate to the apostle Paul's words in *2 Corinthians 4:17*,

> "*For our light affliction, which is but for a moment, is working for us a far more exceeding and eternal weight of glory...*"

My friend, I understand many times we want to escape or avoid the hardships we face in our marriage, but trials have a way of strengthening our relationship with God and our spouse, if we let them. As the apostle Paul proclaimed in *Romans 8:28-29*,

> "*We know that all things* (the good, the bad, and the ugly) *work together for good to those who love God, to those who are called according to His purpose. For whom He foreknew, He also predestined to be conformed to the image of His Son, that He might be the firstborn among many brethren.*"

Every trial we face in life is worth it if we gain a greater reality of God and come into a deep abiding love relationship with our Creator. Jeff and I realized we could have biblical joy amid whatever we had going on because God was building a testimony in us that we could then share with others. Just as, Paul encourages us in *2 Corinthians 3-7,*

> *"Blessed be the God and Father of our Lord Jesus Christ, the Father of mercies and God of all comfort, who comforts us in all our tribulation, that we may be able to comfort those who are in any trouble with the comfort with which we ourselves are comforted by God." (verses 3-4) Now if we are afflicted, it is for your consolation and salvation, which is effective for enduring the same sufferings, which we also suffer. Or if we are comforted, it is for your consolation and salvation. And our hope for you is steadfast, because we know that as you are partakers of the sufferings, so also you will partake of the consolations." (verses 6-7)*

When you take a moment to think about all the saints that have gone before us and the many afflictions they faced, we benefit greatly from their testimony! Just as *Romans 15:4* states,

> *"For whatever things were written before were written for our learning, that we through the patience and comfort of the Scriptures might have hope.*

God has a beautiful way of using every hardship to weave a beautiful tapestry of our lives so that others can detect His fingerprints of love on our story. As we cry out to Him in the day of trouble, He does deliver us, and it becomes an opportunity for us to glorify Him (*Psalm 50:15*).

Take a moment to ask God what He desires to produce in you, so the light of His Son will shine through your life and give hope to others. God's ultimate purpose is that you become a living epistle that all men can read (*2 Corinthians 3:2)*. You can then testify that, "God is real; only He could have transformed my heart and marriage." If God has allowed some trial to come into your marriage don't run from it, my dear sister. Embrace it.

As we conclude this study, I know it has been quite a journey. But I want to encourage you that "*weeping may endure for a night*" and sometimes that night season can seem very long. However, hold onto the promise that "*Joy does come in the morning." (Psalm 30:5)* God has promised us in *Psalm 126:5*, "*They that sow in tears shall reap in joy."* What greater joy can we have if, when we see Jesus face-to-face, He says to us, "*Well done my good and faithful servant"?* In due time, we will all experience what is written in *Revelation 21:4,*

> "*God shall wipe away all tears from their eyes, and there shall be no more death, neither sorrow, nor crying, neither shall there be anymore pain for the former things are passed away."*

Beloved, everything we go through in our lifetime will be worth it all when we see Jesus. That will be our greatest joy of all. Until we meet again.

Write out, meditate, and memorize *Revelation 21:4* for this week.

Learning How to Have Biblical Joy In the Midst of Trials

Today, we will look at the apostle Paul and all that he suffered while he was alive here on earth. In *2 Corinthians 11:24-27* (NIV), Paul declared,

> *"I have been in prison more frequently, been flogged more severely, and been exposed to death again and again. Three times I was beaten with rods, once I was pelted with stones, three times I was shipwrecked, I spent a night and a day in the open seas. I have been constantly on the move. I have been in danger from rivers, in danger from bandits, in danger from my fellow Jews, in danger from Gentiles; in danger in the city, in danger in the country, in danger at sea; and in danger from false believers. I have labored and toiled and have often gone without sleep; I have known hunger and thirst and have often gone without food; I have been cold and naked."*

This same Paul told the church in Philippi,

"For I have learned to be content whatever the circumstances. I know what it is to be in need, and I know what it is to have plenty. I have learned the secret of being content in any and every situation, whether well fed or hungry, whether living in plenty or in want. I can do all things through Christ who gives me strength." (Philippians 4:11-13)

Wow! What a testimony. I would say we have much to learn from this dear saint. Paul said he could go through all those hardships *"through Christ, who gives me strength."*

1. *Read John 15:1-8.* How do you think it was possible for Paul to bear the fruit of contentment amid all he faced according to this passage of scripture?

2. In a Strong's Concordance, look up the Greek definition for *abide*.

3. Read *Act 13:52; Galatians 5:22,* and *1 Thessalonians 1:6.* Where does the fruit of biblical joy come from?

4. What else can you learn about biblical joy according to *Psalm 5:11, Psalm 16:11,* and *Psalm 32:11?*

The joy we read about in these verses is not a giddy feeling, which is here today and gone tomorrow. Nor is it a joy based on perfect circumstances. True biblical joy comes from the Holy Spirit and from abiding in the Vine, moment by moment. It is an inner knowing that, "I am His and He is mine. He is in the center of this storm." Although no one desires to go through hardships, if we are walking in the Spirit then we shall bear the fruit of biblical joy even in the middle of any adversity we face in life. We too, like the apostle Paul, will be able to say, "*For I have learned to be content whatever the circumstances; I can do all things through Christ who gives me strength."*

May you continue to abide in an ongoing relationship with Christ in total reliance upon His Holy Spirit regardless of your circumstances. As you do, allow *'Christ* to *strengthen your heart'* just as He did for the apostle Paul. Take some time to pray through this passage today.

The Joy of the Lord
Is Your Strength

In *Nehemiah 8:10*, Ezra proclaimed to the children of Israel, *"The joy of the Lord is your strength."* This was a people who had seen many miracles in their lifetime, such as the time when God delivered them out of Egypt. Did you ever wonder why Ezra had to remind God's people of this truth when they knew who their God was?

1. Look up the Hebrew word for *joy* and *strength* in this passage of scripture. Write out their definitions.

2. Based on this definition, how would you interpret *"the joy of the Lord is my strength"?*

In the Amplified Bible, *Nehemiah 8:10* reads, *"And be not grieved and depressed, for the joy of the Lord is your strength and stronghold."* Isn't it interesting that God's people can be grieved and struggle with depression? At times, we need to be reminded of that (especially when the storm clouds are passing through our lives) just as the Israelites needed reminding that *'the joy of the Lord is our strength and stronghold'*.

3. Look up *Psalm 21:1; Psalm 27:6,* and *Psalm 43:4* and consider how did the Psalmist deal with these emotions when he faced trials of all sorts.

164

David's love for God is to be deeply admired. His love for His Creator was not based on his circumstances being just right. David loved God unconditionally. Out of that love, he worshipped His Maker with all his might, no matter how he was feeling or what emotion he was struggling with at the time. David was not concerned with what people thought of him *(2 Samuel 6:16-21)*. Whenever he was in God's presence the *joy of the Lord* just came pouring out of his heart.

Think about how many times you have felt as if you were drowning in a sea of sorrow. Praising and giving thanks to the Lord was the last thing on your heart, no doubt. However, when you went to a worship service and began to offer the sacrifice of praise to your Creator, suddenly, the love of God lifted you up out of the miry clay, out of discouragement and despair. Your heart was flooded with so much joy as you thought about all that God has done for you through His Beloved Son. You left that service as if God had given you divine strength inside to keep moving forward. I know this has happened to me in more ways than I could count. *Romans 5:11* tells us,

> *"But we also joy in God through our Lord Jesus Christ, by whom we have now received atonement."*

The *joy of the Lord that is our strength* is knowing Jesus has purchased us with His blood and now we can have peace with God no matter what comes into our lives.

4. Look up *Philippians 3:1* and *Philippians 4:4.* What are we encouraged to do?

When we are facing different fiery trials in our marriage, it is important to practice what Paul stated, "*To rejoice in the Lord and again I say rejoice.*" We can rejoice knowing that on the cross, Jesus has triumphantly overcome everything we face. As you consider Him (*Hebrews 12:2),* may *the joy of the Lord* strengthen your heart each day until you one day see Your Beloved and Blessed Lord face to face.

Spend some time rejoicing in the gift of your salvation. Worship Him with praise music and rehearse the truth of His love for you today.

That Your Joy May be Full

For our final lesson, I would like to look at three biblical accounts in which each situation looked hopeless. First, we will look at Sarai, Abraham's wife. God knew at His appointed time that she would receive much joy because of the fulfillment of a promise the Lord had made to Abraham regarding Isaac. Second, we will look at the children of Israel and the promise God made to them in which He would send a deliverer to bring them out of Egypt. Last, we will look at Jesus, who told His disciples He was going to be arrested, beaten, and crucified on a cross, and yet, on the third day He would be resurrected from the dead.

As you read through these accounts, in every one of their lives they faced a misfortune, calamity, evil affliction, or enduring suffering. Yet, there were many promises that were made to them through God's Word. Just as these individuals had to go through a time of mourning before each promise would be fulfilled in their lives, so do we too.

1. Read *Genesis 18:1-15* and *Genesis 21:1-6.*

2. Read *Exodus 13:18, Exodus 14:16-31, Exodus 15,* and *Psalm 105:43.*

3. Read *John 15:11* and *John 16:20-24.* What was Jesus' desire for His disciples?

Often, during our seasons of weeping we can think the fiery trial that God has allowed to come into our lives is strange. Just as the apostle Peter had to remind the church, we too must be reminded of these things,

> *"Beloved, do not think it strange concerning the fiery trial which is to try you, as though some strange thing happened to you; but rejoice to the extent that you partake of Christ's sufferings, that when His glory is revealed, you may also be glad with exceeding joy. If you are reproached for the name of Christ blessed are you, for the Spirit of glory and of God rest upon you." (1 Peter 4:12-14a)*

Yet, we are encouraged that,

"When His glory is revealed, they may be glad with exceeding joy."

Likewise, in *John 17:13,* Jesus prayed,

"But now I come to You, and these things I speak in the world that they may have My joy fulfilled in themselves."

In the previous chapter *(John 16)*, Jesus told his disciples all the things He and His disciples would have to suffer. But, He gave them a promise. He told them,

"Therefore, you now have sorrow; but I will see you again and your heart will rejoice, and your joy no one will take from you." (John 16:22)

My friend, even though weeping may endure for a night or a season, it is the heart of your Heavenly Father *"That your joy may be full when His glory is revealed." (John 15:11)*

As the disciples faced three dark nights of the soul when Jesus was placed in a tomb, I am sure that the darkness was completely overwhelming. Yet, on the third day, when He triumphantly arose from the grave, each one of those disciples experienced a joy that was inexpressible and full of glory.

As we conclude our final day of this study, the apostle John wrote to the church, *"These things I have written to you, that your joy may be full,"* in the midst of all you are going through. My prayer for you is this: *"May the God of hope fill you with all joy and peace in believing, that you may abound in hope by the power of the Holy Spirit." (Romans 15:13)* Beloved, one day we will look back at all we have gone through during our lifetime here on earth and greatly rejoice because Jesus was with us every step of the way. May you rejoice in that reality. My friend, continue to pray through this trial. Until we meet again.

Week Eight, Day 5, Friday

Personal Application

Review Days 1 through 4 of this week's study and answer the following questions.

1. As you look back on Day 2, identify times when you sensed biblical joy amid all you were going through?

2. How could biblical joy increase in your life based on Day 2?

3. As you reflect on Day 3, have you been struggling with depression as you have been walking through this trial? How do you know?

4. According to Day 3, what can you begin to do biblically to come out of that downward spiral?

5. List five ways you see Jesus filling you with biblical joy and peace?

Conclusion

Dear friends, I never imaged 27 years ago that life with my husband could be what it is today. I am amazed at all God has done over the years in our lives, individually and as a couple, through the various trials we have faced together. At this point, it is almost as if the story I have shared with you throughout this Bible study never existed. God has truly made all things new in our marriage. What I thought was impossible, God has done. As David wrote in *Psalm 30:1-5,*

> *"I will extol You, O Lord, for you have lifted me up, and have not let my foes rejoice over me. O Lord my God, I cried out to You, and you healed me. O Lord, You brought my soul up from the grave; You have kept me alive, that I should not go down to the pit. Sing praise to the Lord, you saints of His, and give thanks at the remembrance of His holy name. For His anger is but for a moment, His favor is for life; weeping may endure for a night, but **joy comes in the morning**."*

Although this was David's testimony, I can certainly say that God has made it our testimony as well.

I am so blessed to be Jeff's wife and to have ministered alongside my husband, in many different capacities over the past twenty-five years. Each time we have an opportunity to minister to a couple, it serves as a reminder to us of the tremendous mercy God has had upon our lives. As we continue to share our story, we have witnessed the Lord give hope to those who are desperate for help in their marriages. Our life story testifies that, *"With God all things are possible,"* since *"Jesus is the same yesterday, today and forever."* I pray that will be your testimony some day.

I would like to leave you with this beautiful prayer the apostle Paul penned from *Ephesians 3:13-21* (Amplified Bible)

> *"So, I ask you not to lose heart [not to faint or become despondent through fear] at what I am suffering in your behalf. [Rather glory in it] for it is an honor to you. For this reason, seeing the greatness of this plan by which you are built together in Christ], I bow my knees before the Father of our Lord Jesus Christ, for whom every family in heaven and on earth is named [that Father from Whom all fatherhood takes its title and derives its name]."*

> *"May He grant you out of the rich treasury of His glory to be strengthened and reinforced with mighty power in the inner man by the [Holy] Spirit [Himself indwelling your innermost being and personality]. May Christ through your faith [actually] dwell (settle down, abide, make His permanent home) in your hearts! May you be*

rooted deep in love and founded securely on love. That you may have the power and be strong to apprehend and grasp with all the saints [God's devoted people, the experience of that love] what is the breadth and length and height and depth [of it];"

"[That you may really come] to know [practically, through experience for yourselves] the love of Christ, which far surpasses mere knowledge [without experience]; that you may be filled [through all your being] unto all the fullness of God [may have the richest measure of the divine Presence, and become a body wholly filled and flooded with God Himself]!"

"Now to Him Who, by (in consequence of) the [action of His] power that is at work within us, is able to [carry out His purpose and] do superabundantly, far over and above all that we [dare] ask or think [infinitely beyond our highest prayers, desires, thoughts, hopes, or dreams]—To Him be glory in the church and in Christ Jesus throughout all generations forever and ever. Amen (so be it)."

For Consideration

As we have concluded our study, I would like to suggest the following assignments for your ongoing spiritual growth while you face various trials in your marriage.

➢ Prayerfully consider going through this study numerous times so that the Holy Spirit can continue to work in your heart in the specific areas we studied during the past eight weeks.

➢ You might want to pick a specific area in which you struggled the most during these eight weeks.

➢ Consider redoing that week's homework.

➢ As you do this, you might want to expand that week's study into your very own Bible study.

➢ Another option: consider going through this study again with other women who might be facing trials in their marriages.

➤ Continue to saturate your mind and heart with the truth of the scriptures. Here are some that you can start with:

> *Psalm 31:24; Psalm 33:18; Psalm 39:7; Psalm 42:11; Psalm 71:5; Psalm 146:5; Jeremiah 17:7; Joel 3:16*

➤ Make sure you are actively involved in a local Bible-discipleship church.

➤ Seek out a sister in Christ who can pray with you on a regular basis as you are walking through this trial.

➤ Keep a journal of God's "fingerprints of love" on your life by writing out a gratitude list on a daily basis.

➤ Continually rehearse God's faithfulness in your life.

➤ Study the attributes of God that are included throughout the scriptures.

Acknowledgements

I would like to thank all my dear friends, who have helped me in editing this Bible study. Tim and Lisa Bates, your love and friendship over the many years have been a precious gift from the Lord to me. Your valuable input and thought-provoking ideas for this study have made it what it is today. To my dear friend, Stacy Morton, I am very thankful for how God put you in my life many years ago for such a time as this. Peggy Meeks and Susan Smith, it has been a blessing to work alongside you while I was employed at Pure Life Ministries and to have you share your valuable input. To Dr. Daniel Berger, II, I thank you for your review of this Bible Study and your valuable insight. To Deborah Lockwood, thank you for your gift of editing that has allowed this study to be ready for publication. Thank you, dear friends for helping me in this endeavor. I could not have done this without your prayer support.

About the Author

Rose Colón serves on the Board of Directors of the Lighthouse Biblical Counseling Center (LBCC) that she cofounded with her husband, Jeff, in October 2015. She is the Director of Women's Counseling and Administrative Assistant to the President of LBCC (lighthousebcc.org).

Lighthouse Biblical Counseling Center (LBCC) exists to teach and train principles from the Holy Scriptures which will allow individuals to live a victorious Christian life, free from the bondage of sin and its consequences. LBCC is also a Training Center for the International Association of Biblical Counselors (IABC.net).

Rose is also a Training Center Director for the International Association of Biblical Counselors in the tri-state area for women who are interested in certification. Rose earned a Master of Ministry in Biblical Counseling from the Master's International School of Divinity and is certified with the IABC as a biblical counselor.

Prior to the formation of LBCC, Rose was employed at Pure Life Ministries (PLM) for 22 years, where she held the position of Director of Women's Counseling for PLM and was a keynote speaker for numerous national and international conferences along with her husband, Jeff.

Recommended Resources

Lighthouse Biblical Counseling Center
www.lighthousebcc.org

International Association of Biblical Counselors
www.IABC.net

Pure Life Ministries, Inc.
www.purelifeministries.org

Healing Hearts Ministries
www.healingheartsministries.org

Revive Our Hearts
www.reviveourhearts.org

Made in the USA
Middletown, DE
11 February 2019